Create Your Blockbuster Life

HOW TO STEP OUT OF THE WINGS INTO YOUR SPOTLIGHT

Deborah Meredith

Contents

For Floss and Boo.

Because dreams really do come true.

Xxx

Create Your Blockbuster Life

I always wanted to write a book. I wrote my first book "Whatever It Takes" and "Create Your Blockbuster Life" was originally part of that. Both books came about because too many people told me "You should write a book" based upon my experiences and I thought 'why not?'

Initially, I wrote as therapy for myself but gradually I started to write for other people, other women who might be going through something similar. Other women who feel or felt so alone in their relationships and think that somehow it's their fault but deep down know that it's not.

I figured that if I was going through this, then surely other people must be going through it too.

I thought I was happily married and was building a UK industry-leading successful business. In just three short years my business had failed, my marriage had ended, I'd been declared bankrupt, I'd been made redundant 3 times and I'd lost custody of my son. I was on the verge of bankruptcy for a second time and had decided it was time to end it all.

In the intervening years I learned that I'd been in a psychologically abusive relationship. Many women in such relationships rarely realise it, and if they do, they don't acknowledge it. It's incredibly hard to prove and many of the professionals in the field don't recognise it until long after any damage has been done. Recovering from what was a form of Post Traumatic Stress Disorder (PTSD), I suffered panic attacks, depression, anxiety and incredibly low self-esteem and lack of confidence.

Picking yourself back up from a metaphorical kick in the teeth or punch in the stomach is hard work and very often it would have been easier to disappear further into the wings and not venture out into the spotlight.

I had no money to invest in coaching, counselling or any other form of help and so I turned to books and the internet to glean what advice I could. I knew I was going to have to help myself and give myself some tough love if I was going to improve and change my life.

Create Your Blockbuster Life, is a collation of the tips and tricks I used to keep myself going and to change my life. It will help you to make gradual changes in your life that will enable you to step out of the wings into YOUR spotlight, whatever that may be.

Everything in this book has been tried and tested by me. I have embraced my philosophy of 'Step Out of the Wings into Your Spotlight' and rewritten my script. 5 years ago I had a plan, at the time I had no idea how to execute that plan but I did it, now I have another plan, another script that will once again take me further into the 'spotlight' of my own life. This book marks the transition from another set of wings into another 'spotlight' and so it will continue but everything I've done has been as a result of following the directions in this book.

It's been hard work, but it's been worth it. There have been plenty of times when I wanted to give up, when things weren't happening fast enough but each time I just followed the directions and kept looking ahead, allowing myself to be drawn into the Spotlight.

Part of my plan included getting a degree and I embarked upon a BSc (Hons) Psychology with Counselling degree with the Open University. The more I have studied and learned on the subject the more I understand and the more I want to help others. My studying has had a huge influence on the direction my life is now taking and forms part of a 5-year plan that will come to fruition when I am 50. Who knew I would one day end up a scientist? I was classed as a science no-hoper in school!

This book is one of a series. I like to think of it like a play, written in Three Acts and a finale or like a film trilogy. "Create Your Blockbuster Life: Step Out of the Wings into Your Spotlight" is Act II, Act III and a Finale. Act I, is my first book, it's my story, my old script. I've outlined the acts below so you can choose whether you wish to just read this book which tells you how to Create Your Blockbuster Life or whether you wish to find out where the story really started and discover the back-story for this book.

Book 1 - Whatever it Takes: Living with, Leaving and Surviving Psychological Abuse

Act I – Lights! - sets the scene. It tells you how this book came about, the experiences I had to go through to get to where I am today and how I believed I was destined to live permanently in the wings, lurching from one bad dramatic tragedy to the next. In short, it shines a light on my past and acknowledges its use in getting me this far and gives me the benefit of lots of lessons gleaned from lots of rehearsal time!

Book 2 - Create your Blockbuster Life: Step Out of the Wings Into YOUR Spotlight

Act II – Camera! - shares the secrets of how I knew that it was time to step out of the wings into the spotlight and how I decided what it would look like when I took that step. I tell you how I created the picture of the life I wanted and how you can do the same too by using the exercises I will share in Act III to help you create the life you really want. It allows you to look through the lens to create the vision you want to see.

Act III – Action! – tells you how to take action and gives you the tools to take the action to move you out of the wings into the spotlight of your life.

Finale – Gives you a glimpse of your happy ending. The happy ending of the script you're writing that will keep you in the spotlight for as long as you desire.

Act II, this book, is about stepping out of the dark shadows of the wings where we've been waiting for far too long and stepping into our spotlight. It's about standing up for ourselves and our beliefs, it's about our passions and our talents. It's about discovering ourselves and finding our voice in whatever form that takes. It's about throwing off the shackles that life has bound us in, opening the curtains wide and taking centre stage. It's about remembering that life is 'Not a Rehearsal' and rediscovering our role in it. Let's step into our spotlight together, the time is now.

My hope is that if you are going through something similar then I want you to feel that you are not alone and you are not to blame. This book is intended to help people like you; who are or have been in psychologically abusive relationships and want to rewrite your script and to create a blockbuster life.

Let's do it together.

ACT II

CAMERA – TAKING A LOOK THROUGH THE LENS TO SET THE VISION FOR THE FUTURE

"I look to the future because that's where I'm going to spend the rest of my life"
George Burns

CHAPTER 1

Identifying What Needed to Change

I had a choice, I could carry on with my original plan to end it all which would mean I wouldn't be here writing this. If I'd followed that plan I would have been dead for almost 8 years by now. Or, I could follow the crazy, ludicrous idea I'd come up with that might just help me out of the situation I was in.

Within a couple of hours, I had created a very basic business homepage. Within 24-hours I had my first client.

This was to be a short-lived business venture but it gave me enough time to put my finances in order, put myself back onto an even keel and find myself a long-term temporary position.

It taught me many, many things about myself, more about human-kind than I ever thought I'd learn, changed many preconceptions and judgements and surprisingly altered my view of the world for the better.

But one thing was certain, I would never be the same again

and the term 'whatever it takes' would take on a completely different meaning but that's a story for another day.

As I've said, that business was short-lived but life-saving.

Within a few months I managed to secure myself a long-term temp position and had shored up my finances once more. I then set about working out what I wanted to achieve in the future.

I had to take a long hard look at myself, my circumstances, identify the lessons, glean what I'd learned and apply it to my future. I also had to change what didn't work and where necessary change myself and my behaviour, but where to start?

It took a lot of reflection, acceptance of some harsh truths and a total change of my mindset to really move myself forward.

The biggest issue I faced was fear. I was absolutely terrified that whatever I turned my hand to I would fail and this proved to be a prophetic consideration. However, I also subscribed to the quote attributed at various times to Albert Einstein, Henry Ford, Mark Twain and Tony Robbins.

"Do what you've always done, you'll get what you've always got."

I knew that I needed to make changes.

One of the things I knew about myself was that I really didn't like being single. I enjoy my own company and my own space but I'm one of those women who prefers to be in a relationship. I'm a natural nurturer and I'm at my happiest when I'm looking after people, not in a mummsying, suffocating way but being able to cook good healthy food for them, laugh with them, cry with them, just be with them; you get the gist. I'm just happier like that, it's in my genes to be a nurturer and surrounded by people. However, I was now in a situation that I really didn't know who to trust and wasn't at all sure who my friends were. I still didn't have the confidence to go and join clubs and associations where I could meet a new set of girlfriends so first things first, I set about writing down *exactly* what I was looking for in a man. I decided this was going to be much easier and I could do it from the security of my own sofa!

In my minds' eye he would be over 6 feet tall, be professional, be prepared to accept that my son, Sam, was part of my life *every* weekend and that that was non-negotiable, he also had to be solvent. There was no way I was going to be the breadwinner for anyone else ever again. I wrote it down as a goal to be achieved and then I put it to one side. I read it every so often but used it more as an aide memoir to remind me what I would and wouldn't accept from the next relationship I entered into. That was all I did but I had a very clear picture in my mind of what that person would be like, without actually knowing what they would physically look like. I knew what qualities I wanted them to have and I knew how we would look when we were out together on a date, I knew how we would interact and I knew how he would get on with my son.

In short, I had visualised and 'seen' every aspect of what our life together would be like and I kept hold of that picture in my mind every time I met a prospective partner.

I applied everything I could learn from people whom I believed 'had it sorted'.

Then I looked at my finances.

Historically, my finances had been somewhat erratic, going through periods of prosperity and then dark periods of relative poverty. I knew I needed to get them in order and so I decided what I needed to achieve, wrote that down as a vision and again, kept reminding myself of it.

In terms of my finances I made lists, lots of lists.

I listed all of my incomings and outgoings. I'd had plenty of experience of cutting back on my spending and living frugally after bankruptcy so I decided to continue to live like that but allowing myself one or two treats per week. I no longer needed to strictly watch every single penny but neither could I run away with myself. I allowed myself to buy the wine I really liked rather than all I could afford and I treated my son and I to an occasional take away or pizza instead of cooking every weekend. I started to buy occasional desserts as well and it made a difference. We both felt like we were having treats and we would excitedly plan what we would eat the following weekend. I started planning meals and visualising what Sam and I would have. I'd plan themed evenings on a Saturday; when the Eurovision Song Contest was on we got dressed up and I prepared a small buffet of international food with something from as many different countries as I could manage. This worked well on two counts; it gave us a treat away from the norm and it encouraged Sam to try new foods in a fun, non-threatening way. It's a bit of a tradition that we still observe to this day if we're not away when the Eurovision is on!

Once again, I planned what I wanted, wrote it down and held that image in my mind's eye.

The hardest part for me to envision was what path my future 'career' was going to take. Did I want to enter full-time employment? Did I want to become self-employed? Did I want to start a business?

I wasn't really sure what I wanted to do but I did know I didn't want to remain working in the temp job I was in and I knew without any doubt that I didn't want to continue in the 'stop-gap' business I had created for myself.

It wouldn't have been good for me to continue down that path, I would probably have ended up ill or dead, and for all the planning I had put into trying to take my own life I now realised that I had far too much to give to others and far too much to live for.

I quickly realised I didn't want to go back into employment. I'd got used to working by my own rules, at hours that worked for me. I've always been more of a night owl than an early bird and getting into an office for 8.30am or 9am was a struggle. For years I'd stated that my perfect office hours would be 11am to 7pm or later, say 1pm to 9pm. I woke up when most people started to wind down. I'd save all of my most important work for the afternoons as that was when I was at my most productive.

I really struggled to be attentive and productive before lunchtime because that wasn't my natural biorhythm.

I decided that I needed to get a job to give me some stability and a regular income for at least a short while so my long-term temp role would fit the bill for the time being but in the meantime I would keep pursuing the self-employment dream and see what opportunities presented themselves. Again, I wrote it down, kept a mental image in my mind and remained open to whatever might happen.

However, I also started to remember my childhood dreams.

What I really wanted was to follow my lifelong dream of becoming a professional actor. I now had the opportunity to change everything and rewrite my script. I registered with an extras agency and started looking for local actors networks and events that I could attend.

The next thing I wanted to address was my health and wellness. I'd been through a period of extreme stress and anxiety. I was also depressed although I never took the medication that the professionals recommended. I wanted to work through this myself without relying on any chemicals.

I'd been neglecting my diet and exercise. In place of food I was drinking far too much wine. Not enough for it to be a problem but too much for me to carry on like that. One bottle a night (or more on some nights) was far too much to carry on indefinitely. I'd stopped eating, something that I'd also done in my late teens when in what I now know was an abusive relationship with the man who became my first husband, but this time, rather than actively stopping eating I'd just forget to eat.

The very same friend I had contacted on that life-saving, life-changing night, would often call me and ask me, "when was the last time you ate?" In one instance we worked out between us that I hadn't actually eaten anything for 3 days, simply because I had forgotten to eat! I just didn't get hungry and if I did get the occasional pang of hunger I would open a bottle of wine earlier than normal and use it to quash my hunger pangs.

This was a worrying and quite destructive behaviour pattern to get into and I knew I needed to make a conscious decision to look after myself.

I have a number of quite severe food allergies and sometimes it was just too much bother to cook some good healthy food for myself so I just wouldn't eat.

I would occasionally binge on crisps and chips which soon became meal replacements with the occasional banana or apple added to the mix. This was a psychological trick to make me think I was being healthy when the reality was I was far from that.

I needed to start looking after myself properly. So, I wrote that down, I created some meal plans, wrote them down, created a shopping list, bought the food and held the vision and feeling in my mind of how much brighter my skin would look, how much slimmer I would feel and how much more energy I would have when I started to nurture myself again.

I also knew that in order to improve my mental health I had to stop giving myself away and stop looking for love through that door marked sex. It wasn't doing me any good emotionally and I knew I couldn't carry on like that.

Deep down I knew I was worth much more than that. I also knew that if a girlfriend was in the same position I would be telling her that she was worth more than that.

I had to start listening to that quiet, tentative voice of my own that had been silenced over the preceding years. It was gradually starting to make itself heard again.

CHAPTER 2

The How and The What

It was pretty easy to identify the areas that I wanted to change and to come up with grandiose ideas of what that change would look like, it was much, much harder to actually look at them through a very critical lens and work out exactly how I would bring about change and bring the vision in my mind to reality.

The first thing I did was identify the areas that I wanted to change and indeed, needed to change. And you've probably already identified them yourself from the previous chapter. These fell into four categories:

1) Relationships or Family
2) Career/Work/Business or Purpose
3) Health and Wellbeing
4) Financial

Within my coaching practice I now refer to them as:

- Supporting cast and crew
- Agent, manager and publicist
- Therapist, personal trainer and chef
- Accountant and Wealth Manager

What I needed to do was to start looking at myself as a business, as THE business and to treat myself in exactly the same way I would treat a business, a client or anyone else.

All too often we are great at helping other people but we neglect ourselves. That airline analogy that I'm sure you'll be familiar with is so true, you have to put your own mask on first so then you are better able to help others. If I didn't start to look after myself first, I wouldn't be able to look after or nurture others which is what truly brought me and continues to bring me joy and happiness. If I wasn't prepared to take control of my own happiness, who was?

I have to admit that this was hard work and as much as I could feel positive and hyped up about my plans, it was much, much easier to remain wallowing in the shallows of my self-pity. I bounced back and forth between feeling confident and feeling terrified but over time I noticed that when I took action, however small, usually only when I was feeling confident, that it would generate results that moved me slightly further forwards. It was much easier to remain rooted to the spot (my sofa) and do nothing, but there was that tiny voice shouting at me from the recesses of mind that if I didn't do something to maintain momentum that I'd be right back where I started and I knew I didn't want that. But, what did I want?

First of all, I needed to audition and recruit my supporting cast and crew. My immediate family were great and they weren't going anywhere. My relationship with Sam, parents, sister and niece were strong and still are. Unfortunately, my closest friends lived the furthest away and whilst we maintained regular telephone contact I hadn't been completely honest with them about how desperate and alone I was feeling. To this day they have no idea how I felt during my bleakest times but I know that if they had known they would have been on my doorstep in next to no time. My pride stopped me from being totally honest with them. My closest friends and closest family had no idea how low I was. I had become so adept at putting on a brave face and playing the confident, outgoing daughter/sister/friend/business owner that it was easier to continue playing that role than to burden anyone with the real me. I knew that she wasn't great company and not easy to be around. It wasn't fair on them I reasoned, to drag them down with me! Besides which, they most definitely wouldn't have liked me. I was making these decisions for them and I had no right to, but I felt I was doing them a favour! But, if I was going to change my life, I had to start with changing myself and I was the only person who could do that.

If that's how you're feeling, don't worry. It's perfectly normal and acceptable to be feeling like that. You're feeling overwhelmed with what you want to do aren't you? That's OK. We're going to work through this together and you're going to get through it. It's just one tiny change at a time, so small that you won't notice you've changed anything until you stop and look back at how far you've come. Trust me, I've been through the process. I've got the t-shirt and I've written the book!

CHAPTER 3

Supporting Cast and Crew Relationships

I had always believed the mantra "Fake it until you Make it" and I knew from my acting experiences that I was very, very capable of playing a role so each morning I got up and did what I envisioned the new, improved me would do and started to develop a relationship with myself.

That was difficult, how can you love someone who doesn't love themselves? Not in a narcissistic way but in a way where they're just happy with who they are. I would look into the mirror and see a wallflower, a shadow of the woman I once was. Quite often I would sit there and cry, grieving for the vibrant, outgoing, full-of-life young woman who once inhabited my body and I'd wonder where she went. Gradually I started to get her back.

For the first few days just showering and doing my hair was a massive step. I have long hair, I've always had long hair and really loved it, but I was at the stage where if it appeared a little greasy I'd just tie it back and tell myself I'd wash it tomorrow. I'd have a wash at the sink and only bath or shower if I was going out. My self-esteem really was that low. But having allowed myself the time to grieve for the woman I once was I reasoned with myself that just showering, doing my hair and putting on a bit of lipstick would brighten me up. I was constantly having to tease myself that this would make me feel better.

Just like an actor puts on a costume and make-up to become a character, I had to do the same to remind myself who the real me was.

It took about two weeks for me to stop feeling self-conscious about showering, doing my hair and putting on make-up just for myself but it was having the desired effect. The better my reflection in the mirror, the happier I felt. Yes, like most women, I was able to find fault and be hyper self-critical but I chose to ignore that voice. Instead, I compared myself with how I'd been a week ago, a month ago and recognised the improvements, acknowledged them and enjoyed them.

This isn't to say that you must wear make-up in order to feel happy about yourself. I'm now at a stage where I'm equally happy bare-faced or with make-up. However, at the time, putting on make-up was something that helped me to regain my confidence, it almost gave me a physical mask to hide behind.

As I started to feel better about myself so my confidence improved and my relationships benefitted. When I was talking to people on the telephone I had more joy in my voice. This was almost imperceptible and I didn't realise it but it was commented on by family and those friends I spoke to on the phone.

My close family noticed that I was more relaxed than I had been for a while. Whilst I had been putting on my 'costume' when I was meeting people my persona had been more extreme than usual, almost becoming a caricature of who I thought they wanted me to be.

As my confidence grew in tiny amounts so my character became more authentic. There was still a long way to go but more of the real me was starting to get through. The neural pathways were waking up slowly and 'me' started to drip through my veins. There was still a very long way to go and it would be a number of years before I really shed my skin but I was on the right track.

With my new-found, albeit minimal confidence, I decided it was time to actively search for a partner rather than just pay it lip-service.

I didn't have the confidence to actually go out to pubs or restaurants on my own and I was very nervous about joining a dating website, having been on one previously and not having very good results.

I had read a lot about finding your perfect partner and subscribed to visualising your dreams for most other areas of my life so I decided I had nothing to lose and I wrote out exactly what I was looking for in a partner as mentioned in the previous chapter. In short, he had to be solvent, kind and loving. He had to treat me like a Princess and Sam like his own.

I had no idea how I was going to meet such a man when I wasn't prepared to utilise the only methods I thought were available but I didn't let that stop me. I wrote it down, re-read it occasionally, committed it to memory and started to use it as a checklist whenever I met anyone who was potentially suitable. I even asked myself "What would Julie do?"

Julie was, and is, my closest girlfriend. I was always teasing her about how harsh she was on potential partners. I thought she frightened them off with her demands but I realised that this was more about her own self-esteem than trying to be horrible or stand-offish. She only wanted a partner who could give her what she felt she deserved in relationship terms.

It took a while but I met the person I would then go on to spend two and a half years with by applying my criteria. I met him at a networking event which I'll explain shortly!

Around this time I had also started to become very interested in the 'personal development world'.

Having always been a voracious reader I was reading as many free and low-cost books and reports as I could get my hands on. I came across Neale Donald Walsh's book 'When Everything Changes, Change Everything' and I pretty much took the title literally which you'll discover as you read this section.

At the networking event I saw a tall, well-dressed, confident man chatting to a group of people, one of whom I actually knew. I didn't know anyone else in the room. I went over to join the group, standing next to the person I knew, gradually I was drawn into the conversation and the man I spotted handed me his business card and suggested we had a coffee sometime.

As is the case with networking events, we soon each moved on to talk to other people but I was aware of him looking over at me on a couple of occasions (only because I caught him doing so as I was looking over at him!) Before long we were in the same group again, the event was drawing to a close and he shook my hand and asked me to call him to arrange a coffee.

This is quite common in networking when you want to find out more about what someone is doing so I found nothing strange about it. The only thing I didn't like was that I didn't have any business cards so I hadn't been able to give him one of mine. The ball was well and truly in my court! Could I really call him? Could I really be that forward? Of course, he didn't know I had an ulterior motive and it was more than coffee I was interested in!

I drove home from the event kicking myself, wishing I'd suggested we had stayed on and had a glass of wine. It was a beautiful spring evening, the hotel the event was at was in a fabulous setting and I could visualise a lovely evening over a glass of wine on the terrace however, it wasn't to be. I wouldn't drink and then drive and I really didn't have the courage to be that forward. Instead I drove home remonstrating with myself for not taking action. He did after all seem to fit all of the criteria I had set so what was stopping me?

I arrived home, changed into my dressing gown, poured myself a glass of wine and settled down in front of the TV. I couldn't focus on the programme that was on, my stomach was churning. This man had caused me to have butterflies in my stomach and I couldn't stop thinking about him.

I decided to send him a text which read something along the lines of, "Lovely to meet you this evening. Would have been nice to enjoy a glass of wine on the terrace whilst continuing to chat. Instead I'm having a glass now whilst overlooking the sea from my window."

I felt that was enough to encourage a response if he wanted an excuse but wasn't so forward as to suggest anything more than a chat. I couldn't believe it when I received a response less than 10 minutes later. We ended up texting late into the night and he said he'd call me the following day.

The following morning, I took extra care about getting myself ready. I had a spring in my step that hadn't been there for a very long time and I had that nervous/excited feeling in my stomach that you get in the early days of a relationship or before a first date. Remember what that feels like? Wouldn't it be incredible to be able to recreate that in your existing relationship?

All of this just on the promise of a telephone call!

If he didn't call we had had a lovely text conversation the night before and some mild flirtation. It had made me feel good and that was all I needed. I congratulated myself with the fact that I hadn't had a one-night stand and yet he still wanted to call me.

For me, this was a major breakthrough!

By mid-morning I still hadn't received a call and was starting to feel let-down. My feelings of unworthiness started to creep back and that little voice inside my head was saying "of course he's not interested in you, he's far too good for you, he doesn't want a washed-up 'has been' on his arm, he's looking for a gorgeous young 20-something who will hang on his every word."

Do you ever do this? As women, particularly as women of certain age, we find ourselves doing this all the time. Talking to ourselves in a horribly negative manner that we'd never ever use when talking to our friends. If you're anything like me you'll know exactly what was going on in my mind!

I was doing a really good job of berating and belittling myself until my telephone rang.

It was him! By this time, I was so down about myself that I was quite short with him on the phone until he asked if I was OK and was I available for lunch. He would be in area at lunchtime and would like to buy me lunch. I lied and told him I was distracted by reading an email and told him that yes, I would be available at lunchtime following a meeting I was about to go into but he could meet me afterwards.

I told him the venue and we arranged to meet.

From then on things moved quite quickly, almost at breakneck speed and we were almost inseparable from that lunch date onwards. He ticked every box on my criteria list which could have been written solely with him in mind it was so uncannily accurate. We met almost 3 months after I had written down what I wanted, visualised it and put it out to the Universe. I would soon learn that I needed to be more specific but for now I had a relationship with exactly the sort of man I had asked for. His name was Michael.

We quickly worked out our groove, every relationship has one, and it was only a few short weeks before he had moved in with me into my cliff-top maisonette. Michael developed a fabulous relationship with Sam and I felt like all of my dreams had come true.

For the most part this was the ideal relationship and on the face of it anyone would have agreed and said I had the perfect relationship. The reality was quite different. Whilst yes, he was solvent, treated me like a princess and developed a good relationship with Sam he was also quite controlling, not as overtly as my ex-husband but to a degree where I soon began to feel stifled and suffocated by the relationship.

He didn't like me going out with the few friends I had as he was worried I would meet someone more deserving of me. I understand now that this was his issue and his lack of confidence and self-belief being projected onto me but at the time I wasn't aware of it and it was easier to decline invitations and play the 'dutiful wife'.

He was quite controlling financially as well. He suggested that as I had been bankrupt all of my income should be paid into his account then he would give me a monthly allowance. Again, on the face of it this was ideal but it also meant that I had to account to someone else exactly what I was spending my money on. Not that I was spending it on anything frivolous or things I shouldn't be buying but I didn't have the freedom that I was used to. It also meant that he would quite often say "I can buy you that" leaving me feeling that he was 'buying' me. I very quickly felt that I was in a conditional relationship, where outwardly he was showing signs of loving me and treating me like a princess, buying me pretty much anything I wanted or asked for but it also meant that if I declined his advances for any reason, he would immediately ask, "Don't you love me anymore? Is there someone else?" This became very wearing and before long I was questioning whether or not he really was my perfect partner.

Old habits die hard and once again I found myself in a relationship that I knew was wrong. I ignored the niggling little voice in the back of my head telling me that and just put up with it. Have you ever done that? I think we all do it at times, ignore that inner voice or gut instinct

I looked at all the material belongings we had, beautiful house, nice cars (he'd bought me a convertible), lovely clothes, good holidays, we ate out often, we had good food at home and most of all we were a family.

I constantly shushed that little voice telling myself I was being ungrateful but in the back of mind I was asking myself, "Why wasn't I happy? Why was I so ungrateful? 'Isn't this what a perfect relationship looks like?"

For the first time in my life I was in a relationship that I couldn't get out of. I couldn't afford to leave as I had no access to any money other than my 'allowance'. I couldn't pull together the deposit I would need for a flat. I told myself to just put up with it, to shut up and stop being ungrateful.

However, I also told myself that life would be different if I was with Alun, an old boyfriend who I hadn't seen but had thought of often over the 12 years or so since we'd split up. I think most of us have 'one who got away' don't we? Alun was mine..

Alun was the love of my life. We'd met when I was 28 and split up when I was 29, drifting apart when our relationship became long-distance and we couldn't make it work. That was long before everyone owned a mobile phone and had internet access. Facebook and Skype didn't exist then!. We were both pursuing new dreams and that was that. I was heart-broken but moved on, as did he.

My friends thought I was crazy when I kept telling them that one day we'd end up together, I had no idea when, where or how but I knew, just knew without doubt, that we were destined to be together.

In the meantime, I'd got married, had Sam and got divorced and my life took an altogether different path to the one I believed I'd have had if Alun and I had stayed together.

As far as I knew Alun was travelling the world and the last I had heard was living in Canada with his girlfriend. I remember exactly where I was when I heard that news. I was at that point still married and Sam was two years old. My business was at the height of its success and I was actively involved in all sorts of business initiatives, networking events and anything else that could promote my business. I'd bumped into Alun's brother whilst I was involved in a Dragons' Den style event being held in the offices where his brother worked. I was one of the dragons. We exchanged pleasantries and when he told me the news about Alun my stomach lurched.

I couldn't explain why I felt so sad and so hopeless but that's how I felt. It had been years since I'd actively thought about him, thinking that ship had long since sailed and I also chose to focus on the marriage that I had rather than what might have been. I kept reminding myself that the grass isn't always greener! But that chance meeting with his brother rekindled all of my old feelings and I knew with absolute certainty that if he was to turn up on my doorstep then I would walk out of my marriage to be with him, however fleetingly that might be. But that was all I heard of him for a number of years although I would be lying if I didn't admit to having since searched for him on Facebook at least twice!

So here I was trapped in the 'perfect' relationship. I was 40 years old and feeling disappointed. 'Is this all there is to life?' I know I'm not the only one to have ever felt like that. Is that how you feel too? Sometimes having it all isn't really what you want at all is it? But how are we meant to deal with that? We're told that the goal is to 'have it all' yet when we get it all we're still not happy. And that's the point of this book, having it all is all about what makes YOU happy, no-one else. It's OK not to want the same things as anyone else. I love doing things that you'd really hate just as you love doing things that I wouldn't enjoy.

I felt like my life was over and I was resigned to living the rest of my days in a relationship that seemed perfect on the outside but really wasn't. I found myself looking at married friends and acquaintances and asking myself if their relationships were genuinely as perfect as they appeared. Was everyone just pretending? Was everyone just settling? Is this what life was really all about? Do you feel like that too?

These questions plagued me not just for days, but for years. I was a child of the 70's having gone to school in the 80's. I was a Thatcher's child. I wanted it all and I was adamant I was going to get it. Why couldn't I live my life on my terms? Was everyone just 'acting as if' and donning the costumes and playing the roles that society dictated? Are you doing that, playing a role that has been dictated to you? Doing what other people have told you that you should do?

During this period, I was undertaking some acting work, I was fortunate and appeared in Casualty, Being Human, Broadchurch and featured in a couple of adverts.

I was also cast in a small touring production of a play. My dream of becoming an actor was finally starting to become a reality.

I was massively excited. Theatre was and is my love and my forte, I love being on a stage. I come alive and feel at home. And it was during rehearsals for this production that Alun came back into my life. Was another dream about to come true?

CHAPTER 4

A Surprise Meeting

Alun was living in one of the towns we would be performing in and had recognised my face on the poster in the theatre when he was booking tickets for another production. He had tracked me down and we'd spoken via Facebook messenger. Nothing major, just catching up as you would an old school friend. I had no idea why he was suddenly contacting me out of the blue and I certainly wasn't going to let him know how I'd felt about him all these years. At this point I had no idea if he was married, single or what was going on. I wasn't about to risk losing my 'perfect' relationship to get my heart broken again, no matter how imperfect my relationship actually was. But inside I was a bundle of nerves and excitement.

Alun and I arranged to meet for a coffee one day after rehearsal.

Within five minutes of meeting at a very central and busy location I knew I was in trouble. Only one other person knew I was meeting Alun and I quickly excused myself to the toilet, locked myself in a cubicle and sent a text to my friend.

It read, "Oh F*%k! I'm in trouble."

Suffice to say all of the old feelings came flooding back and

I knew that whatever happened I couldn't and wouldn't stay in my current relationship. Not that I admitted that right there and then.

Alun told me why he had got in contact, he was single and had always regretted us splitting up and hoped there might be a chance we could get back together one day. I told him I was happy where I was and was not about to give everything up on a whim. It was a very adult conversation with no impropriety, other than a hug and a peck on the cheek.

But it seemed the Universe had other ideas!

Less than a week later, on opening night of my play, my 'perfect' partner, Michael, stormed into the kitchen wanting to know who Alun was. I asked what he was talking about and he said.

"I checked your Facebook. Who the f*%k is Alun?"

I was incredulous. Now he wasn't even hiding the fact that he was checking up on me!

I had intended having a conversation with him about the state of our relationship, me and Alun but was selfishly waiting until after opening night. Michael on the other hand was adamant we were going to discuss it there and then. I implored him to wait until Sunday evening when Sam would have returned to his father's home but he just refused.

Things got quite ugly from there and I'm not going to go into the nitty gritty here. It ended up with me calling Alun and asking him to come and collect me and Sam and take us to my mother's house. Michael had by this time taken all of the car keys off me and had locked me and Sam inside the house, he was becoming increasingly irate and angry to a degree I had never seen before.

I was scared and Sam was scared.

I had to call the one person who I truly believed would look after me without judgement. That person was Alun.

Within three weeks I had moved lock, stock and barrel into his bachelor pad some 35 miles away. Who would you call if you were in that position?

It's fair to say that this wasn't the most conducive start to a new relationship and whilst I was finally with the love of my life, it caused no end of problems in my relationship with my ex-husband who hasn't spoken to me since that day.

Whilst I must admit that I quite enjoy him not talking to me it's not fair on Sam who is now his father's messenger. I actively insist upon calling his father to have important conversations with him about how our son is doing but he refuses to talk to me. He doesn't even acknowledge my existence! However, on the whole, his father's behaviour has strengthened the already strong bond between Sam and myself, so I have no regrets.

Whilst I had always had a dream of who my future partner would be I didn't dare to believe it even though I knew without doubt it was always going to happen. Since then I've learned that nothing is impossible and have even become a certified Law of Attraction practitioner.

The key to manifesting your dreams is to truly believe in them. If you believe, deep down in the pit of your stomach and with all your heart, that it's going to happen, then it really will. I ALWAYS knew I'd end up with Alun even when it seemed impossible. That belief never wavered and there were a number of times when friends tried to talk me out of it. My best friend, Julie, even now says how she thought I needed help and was getting quite worried with my obsession that I would end up with Alun! To quote the song "Don't Stop Believing"!

After this, I was able to sit down and create a clearer vision of the relationship I would like with my parents, my sister and my friends. Relationships take time and energy. They don't work if you try to impose yourself, your views or your opinions on other people. They do work if you're yourself, if you're open, honest and allow your strengths and your vulnerabilities to show through.

For me, it was about changing the person I am in terms of how I felt about myself and allowing me, the real me, to engage with people.

It's still a work in progress but it helped me to create the vision of how I want my future relationships to be.

What do you want your relationships to look like? Not just your romantic relationships but all of your relationships? With family, friends, children, colleagues? What changes to you want to make? What works well? What needs to improve?

CHAPTER 5

Agent, Manager and Publicist - Work/Career

Remember I said that I was changing everything? I jumped ahead and told you that I'd met Alun, However, for now I'm taking you back to when I'd just met Michael and we were still in the first flush of romance. At that stage I believed that I'd sorted my relationship now I needed to work on work.

As my confidence in myself was growing so I decided that I would actively try to get some sort of stable income. I really didn't want to return to the world of employment and I sat down trying to work out a pattern from my previous experiences and my skill set. I could also still hear the words of my former contact and client when he asked me to join him as a Business Consultant. "Your experience is worth far more to me than someone with a certificate who's just read about it."

With this in mind, I decided to reinvent myself as a business coach. I knew from my own experience of hiring a business coach that I had found it difficult to take advice from someone who just knew about business from a book rather than having been through it themselves so I decided that would become my new business.

The irony of that situation is that I felt like such a fraud because I hadn't properly dealt with the feelings of failure of my first business and my subsequent bankruptcy which meant that I didn't believe in myself and really couldn't see how anyone would want to do business with me.

It's true that if you don't believe in what you're doing, you won't succeed at it. We do that a lot don't we? We carry on doing what we're doing even though we know it's not going to change anything. Deep down hoping that one day, something different will happen but not actually doing anything different. Is that what you do too?

Looking back, I now know that with that mind-set I was doomed as a business coach but it's what got me out of the house and through the door to a couple of networking events so it served its purpose to a small degree.

I find it quite amusing now that I used to attend networking events, playing the role of a business coach whilst deep down being terrified that someone might genuinely want to work with me. I had some serious issues!! It was time to focus on what I wanted, what I really wanted AND what I needed.

If you've ever felt like that about something, or are currently feeling that way about something, then it's a pretty clear indicator that you need to change that something.

Once again, I knew I didn't want to go back to be an employee but I also knew I needed to earn some money whilst planning what I was going to do on a self-employed basis. I looked at my CV, looked at my skill-set and decided to approach a temping agency I had worked with on various occasions over the years. I told them I was looking for a medium to long term temping role that would offer me some consistency in terms of pay and accept some flexibility so that I could continue to do some acting work.

I wasn't sure I would get such a role but if it did exist I wanted to be in with a chance of getting it. And I had already learned that if you want something, you need to ask for EXACTLY what you want. I hadn't yet learned to be completely SPECIFIC about what I wanted!

Within a couple of weeks, I was offered a temping position, initially it was to last for around 6 weeks. I accepted it thinking it would give me 6 weeks more pay than I had at the moment (which was zero) and it gave me a little more time to work out what I was going to do next. By the time the 6 weeks was over I had some more extra acting work coming in and I was pretty solvent for a short while. I was also by getting my monthly allowance from Michael so I didn't need to worry too much about an income, but for my own peace of mind I wanted to earn my own money.

Before finishing the 6-week contract I cheekily mentioned to the company that I would be becoming a self-employed PA within the next couple of weeks and if they wished to use me again they could do so if they contacted me directly. I told them my fees and then went off to have some fun in acting roles for a while. I knew that the company had lots of ongoing work and that they liked what I was delivering for them. With the type of work I was doing I also knew that continuity was beneficial so they wouldn't have to retrain someone else. It was worth being cheeky even though I really didn't want to become a PA again if I could help it but it was all that I knew. Anything was better than nothing at all, right?

Soon enough I received a call asking if I was available to go back to the company and do some more temping. I ended up staying there, on and off, for just over a year. Whilst it wasn't exactly what I wanted to do it was a step back on to the self-employed ladder and gave me the flexibility to undertake various acting jobs and Extras work that presented itself.

I had a problem though, although I was now back in the self-employed sphere, I still didn't have the confidence to get out and start coaching, which is what I felt pulled towards and driven by. I still do, you'll be glad to hear although I now have more confidence and more experience than I had at the time. And it's not just life experience that I've got. I've been studying for a BSc (hons) in Psychology and Counselling with the Open University to give me a greater understanding of the theory around why we do the things we do. I've also attended various coaching and personal development courses and seminars too.

But there was a downside; the longer I stayed in the job, albeit self-employed, I was moving further away from my goal and my confidence in my ability to actually achieve my goal and become a coach was ebbing away fast. In addition to this I was contending with a partner who would tell me he was supportive of me doing anything I wanted to do "as long as I didn't give up the work I was doing as we needed the money!"

I got to the stage where I hated the temp job. I felt it was holding me back from doing what I really wanted and I recall saying to Michael that I felt like I was being pimped out for the money. I woke up every morning saying, "I really can't go back there" and he would pull some clothes out of the wardrobe for me, turn the shower on, haul me out of bed and say, "Yes you can, we need the money."

Resentment was starting to set in big time, particularly because I couldn't understand where our money was going. We were still in my flat and I knew the outgoings were relatively low. My income alone would cover those and whilst we had a good lifestyle, I couldn't understand where an additional £3000 a month (from his salary) was going.

However, this didn't stop me from researching the opportunities that were available and before long I stumbled across a personal development group for women that was looking for franchise leaders. I applied and went along to their discovery day and before long I was being offered a franchise. Michael was supportive but also very nervous he didn't like taking risks, but I insisted that I wanted to take the opportunity I was offered.

I remember thinking at the time that something didn't feel right, I didn't feel a connection with the company's owners, but I had so many positive messages from women already involved in the franchise, either as leaders or members, that I ignored my gut instinct and handed over the few thousand pounds it took to purchase my franchise licence.

Once again, I was doing what I felt I should rather than listening to that voice at the back of my head and listening to my gut instinct. Do you find yourself doing this? Often when we're desperate to get out of a situation we don't like, we make the wrong choices. Sometimes we're aware we're doing it but often we don't realise it until much further down the line. If you have read my first book, "Whatever It Takes", you'll find plenty of examples of me doing this so don't worry, you're not alone. And the good news is we can change that.

With a sense of trepidation mixed with elation I set about developing this exciting new business which I felt sure would take me closer to my goal even if something didn't feel quite right. It was tough. It was as if the people I was approaching could sense my uncertainty about it and didn't want to be involved.

Within 3 months I had decided I couldn't be involved in this particular franchise any more. There was a lack of integrity about it that really bothered me. From where I was sitting it was all about getting as much money as possible out of people and not about helping them. I was appalled that we were being advised to make people feel guilty if they weren't signing up to the next programme and being advised to tell them that they didn't value themselves if they weren't prepared to spend the money on their own personal growth and development.

Whilst I accepted that there was an element of that linked to self-worth, I also knew from my own experience that if someone said they couldn't afford it, it was generally because they couldn't afford it. I wasn't prepared to 'bully' people into buying something that would ultimately make their financial situation worse and thus raise their anxiety levels. I submitted my resignation and walked away.

I was threatened with legal action to which my response was, "That's fine, I'll go the press", they tried another angle and I threatened to make myself bankrupt again to which they responded, "You can't do that." "Yes, I can." I replied. "I've done it before and it didn't hurt. It was inconvenient but I survived." They weren't quite sure where to go from there and used all sorts of NLP (neuro-linguistic programming) techniques to try to get me to see their point of view and acquiesce to their demands.

I had heard of NLP and knew from talking to other people that it could get great results but to see it being used in such a devious manner appalled me. I realised that this had been what I had sensed before purchasing the franchise but hadn't been quite so aware of it. To this day I have massive difficulty trusting anyone who tells me they are an NLP Coach or Master Practitioner. However, as part of my ongoing training I have undertaken an NLP course myself so that I can understand how to use it properly and apply it to help the people I work with to create positive change. Studying it alongside my psychology degree I can see that the roots of NLP are based in the science of psychology and it is indeed a very effective tool. Unfortunately, like many things that work well, there will also be a small minority that use it for their own financial gain rather than to improve the lives of the people it was developed to help. I promise you that I will never use NLP in that way. To me, it's just part of a tool kit that I can draw upon to help me help you. It's not the only tool in the box.

I took this set-back very badly. Even though walking away had been my choice, I hadn't anticipated the threats that followed. For all my unease about the franchise, I believed I was dealing with business people who had a few principles. I had used everything I had, both emotionally and financially, to become involved with this franchise and all the feelings of failure, shame, despair and unworthiness came back in quite a dramatic fashion.

My time was once again my own (a nicer way of saying I was unemployed) so I had driven to my local town to collect some dry-cleaning for Michael, a perfectly mundane, routine task. Whilst driving around trying to find a parking space I could sense myself getting tense, my anxiety levels started to rise, my breathing became quicker and shallow and my temperature rose quite dramatically. I know now that I was experiencing my first panic attack. It was awful.

I ended up in such a state at not being able to find a parking space that I drove part of the way home, pulled the car over, got out and ran/walked the rest of the way home. When I got to my flat I locked the door behind me, fell onto my kitchen floor, curled up in a ball, called Michael and sobbed into the phone "you've got to come back, now, I can't do it, I just can't do it." He was working some 35-40 miles away and not being able to get any sense out of me arrived home just over an hour later to see me still curled up on the kitchen floor a snivelling, shaking mess.

Not only had I failed at yet another business, I had failed to be a good partner to Michael. The negative self-talk going on inside my head was loud and clear "I was useless, hopeless and good for nothing. I couldn't do anything right and I needed Michael to help me live a normal life". Echoes of my previous marriage were all around and the Cycle of Abuse was continuing to impact my life.

In "Whatever It Takes" I demonstrate the 'Cycle of Abuse' and you will find an illustration of it in the back of that book if you want further information. In short, I was repeating patterns from earlier in my life which were still having a negative impact on me.

If you feel that this is something you do then please be reassured that it's possible to change it, IF you want to change it and I would recommend you read "Whatever It Takes" as well as this book to help you gain some clarity.

I would stay like that on my kitchen floor for some weeks. Trying to tuck myself further into the corner if someone knocked the front door, ducking down with my hands over my head if I saw someone walk past the window, and jumping as if I had an electric shock every time my phone rang. The franchise company were calling me up to 10 times a day and I was feeling threatened and intimidated by them. It was another very low moment and I felt that I'd taken two steps forward and 100 steps back. My confidence was back through the floor and those old suicidal fantasies were starting to creep back in. I felt stupid, hopeless, a total failure and worthless.

I kept telling myself that I had convinced Michael to allow me to buy the franchise and now he was going to say, "I told you so" just as my ex-husband had about my previous business failure.

I was looking for someone to blame for my own stupidity. I was angry with myself for getting myself back into a similar situation. Angry for having another business failure and angry for choosing the wrong partner again.

I decided I couldn't trust myself anymore and gave myself up to him, allowing him to make all of the decisions for me and guide me to become a much better person. I truly thought I was incapable of doing anything without asking for his input, guidance or permission. I'd just proven to both him and I that I couldn't be trusted with anything financial so it was much better to allow him to take control. I felt I had no choice but to become a 'Stepford Wife'. If you've never watched the film, I recommend you do. It's an interesting take on human psychology and how we allow ourselves to be manipulated by the media, gender stereo-types and society's expectations.

This certainly wasn't the vision I'd created in my mind's eye when I purchased the franchise and I certainly hadn't visualised me failing at it but funnily enough neither had I seen me succeeding at it! I'd spent a lot of time trying to work out why I didn't feel good about the franchise and it's almost as if I hadn't dared to dream I could be successful at anything and in doing so had inadvertently planned my own failure.

What was it I said earlier about truly believing in your dreams if you actually want them to manifest!

Again, somehow, I had to pick myself back up and get back out there.

Around the same time as buying this franchise I had been contacted by an acquaintance who was about to launch her own business. A women's business network. She was planning a grand launch in a prestigious location and invited me to attend. I really didn't feel like attending, I wasn't in the mood and I didn't think I had a business that would be of interest to other attendees.

However, Michael suggested it would do me good to get back out and network and possibly catch up with people I used to know and hadn't seen for a long time. And having decided that he knew best as I couldn't possibly make decisions for myself I allowed him to drive me to the door of the venue. I recall feeling physically sick as I got out of the car, it took me at last three attempts to close the car door and walk into the venue on my own. The panic attacks were subsiding with the use of the beta-blockers I had been prescribed to suppress them but I was still feeling highly stressed and anxious

I walked into the venue where I was warmly welcomed by my acquaintance and quickly introduced to lots of other people.

I remember feeling overwhelmed and switching into 'actor' or 'performance' mode which is my coping mechanism for when I feel out of my depth. I don't really remember much about the evening other than feeling like a complete fraud and wondering what on earth I was doing there. Towards the end of the event, in the closing speeches, my friend, from her position behind the lectern on the stage said she was going to ask a few people to share their experiences and what they hoped to achieve from joining her network. I sat back expecting there to be a handful of ready-primed women in the 250-strong audience who would add credibility to her work and the value of her network.

Within seconds the name of someone I knew was called out and right on cue she stood up and shared with everyone. She was vibrant and full of confidence. I was very impressed and wished I had the confidence she had. As she sat down so I heard my name being called. To my horror I was now being expected to get up and do the same. In that moment I knew I had to make a choice; I could either refuse to get up, embarrass my friend and myself in front of all of those women or I could stand up, put on my best performance face and trust that the right words would come.

I chose the latter.

To this day I have no idea what I actually talked about, I think it was something to do with bankruptcy and how it can affect any one at any time and my mission was to help others not to feel alone, afraid or ashamed of going through a similar situation.

I sat back down to applause and just willed the ground to swallow me up. I couldn't wait for it to be over and I couldn't wait to leave. Surreptitiously I sent a text message to Michael "come and get me NOW". I felt sick and wasn't sure my legs would get me back out of the event to the door. I'd been embarrassed enough, I didn't want to embarrass myself further by throwing up or collapsing in front of everyone. I knew I shouldn't have gone. I hated Michael at that point for making me go. I wanted this performance to end so that I could take off my costume and make up and curl up on my sofa in my dressing gown.

Who was I trying to kid? I'd never be good enough for anything.

CHAPTER 6

Useless or Useful?

At the networking event that I hadn't wanted to attend and had ended up with me willing the ground to open up and swallow me, something strange happened. The event finished and people started to drift off. Some heading straight out, others lingering and catching up with people they knew but some people were coming over to me. I was desperately trying to hide and fade into the background, thinking that by pushing myself closer to the wall I would become invisible. No such luck! People still saw me and came over to me. The chatter in my head was saying 'This is it, they're going to tell me what the heck was I talking about and why on earth did she pick on me when I was rubbish?'

But they didn't. These people were 'actually' commending me on my talk.

They liked it.

They were inspired and motivated by it and they congratulated me on having the strength and courage to stand up and talk so eloquently about it!!

I was confused. They 'actually liked me? They actually thought I gave a good talk? It was going to take some time to sink in.

Have you ever found yourself in a position like this? Maybe in a meeting at work or at a PTA event in your child's school, or at a public meeting where you just knew you needed to have your say then felt horror and remorse at getting up and saying what you said and thought so publicly? You've had your say and then replaying it in your mind you hear that little voice saying, "Why did I say that?" "I sounded so stupid." "What will people think?" "I'll never be able to show my face there again." You know how it is. I think we've all felt like that at some stage in our life, haven't we?

The following day I received a call from my friend. She was grateful for my input into her evening, she had excellent feedback from my talk and would like to meet for a coffee to see if we could work together. "Is this what happens when you follow your purpose?" I questioned myself, self-doubt still raging within. I still wasn't really sure if I had what it took to be a coach but I'd just had feedback that I was a good speaker and could move and inspire people. That was a start. I arranged to meet her for coffee.

In a case of recent history repeating itself I was asked if I would be interested in working with her to help grow her network and develop it to become a franchise. Perhaps I'd even be interested in taking on a franchise myself? We discussed it further and I agreed to work with her. She didn't have the funds to pay me but instead we worked out a way in which I would give her so many hours of administrative support in return for the cost of a franchise, and we identified the franchise I would take over a few months down the line.

In the time we worked together she spent an awful lot of time telling me which way my future career should go. Some of the suggestions I refused outright, others I took on board to some level but all of the time I had that old familiar niggle in the pit of my stomach. And we know what happens when we ignore those niggles don't we? Read on if you want to find out, alternatively, jump straight to the next chapter because you can probably fill in the rest of this one for yourself!

Something wasn't right. I didn't know what it was but I knew that I wasn't happy with it. However, given that she was successful, at least she came across as successful and had the material possessions that exuded success, I decided that once again I didn't know what I was talking about. I couldn't trust myself based on my previous experience and I would just listen to her and Michael who was encouraging me to become more and more involved.

Before long, after assisting her business with both administrative support and some speaking slots as well as some creative input, the night came where we would announce that I would be taking over the next franchise. As she let the gathered audience know that she was about to launch her network and detailed its geographic location, I prepared myself to stand up and share my excitement to be taking it on and my hopes for its future growth and our continued working relationship. As she said, "I'd like to introduce you to the new franchise holder," I surreptitiously moved my chair back and prepared to get to my feet. But she didn't call my name. She mentioned the names of two ladies whom she had told me had bought the franchise for the next town. I couldn't believe what was happening!

Once again, she had managed to make me feel stupid in front of a large audience (not that any of them knew I was taking on the franchise, we'd kept the skill-share agreement private). I could feel my face burning and the sick feeling returning.

I told myself that it didn't matter anyway, they all knew me as the jam and chutney lady and wouldn't possibly take me seriously as the owner of a business coaching franchise. Alongside the temp position and the previous franchise, I had created a jam and chutney business to bring some money in. It was a hobby turned business and although I'd had to become registered as a food business I had no plans to develop it into anything bigger than a cottage-industry that I ran from my own kitchen. I thoroughly enjoyed making the products and selling them at food festivals and farmers markets but I hated stinking of sugar, vinegar and onions on a permanent basis. I consoled myself with the fact that all the people at the event just thought of me as the jam lady who occasionally 'helped out' the network owner by sharing some of my previous experience.

I went home and fell apart once more. How many more times was I going to be a failure? How many more times were people going to take me for granted? I couldn't handle this anymore. Enough was enough.

Once again survival instinct kicked in. I worked out how much money my time was worth and submitted an invoice for her. She refused to pay it and came back with a trite response that denied that any agreement had been in place, even suggesting that for the support she had given me she should be charging me for sharing her expertise and NLP skills. She had completely taken advantage of me being in a vulnerable state and once again I heard that phrase NLP. Michael was equally as angry and it's fair to say some words were exchanged between us. He tried to reason with her on my behalf and he too got nowhere.

I've since learned that I'm not the only person to have suffered the same treatment at her hands and that other women she worked with were also made promises along the lines of skill-swaps, that were then ignored. They too were dropped when she no longer had a use for them. As far as I'm aware that network hasn't grown beyond the original group that I spoke at on the night it launched but the concept was good and I hope that its members are achieving massive success by being part of it.

As for the previous franchise, the self-development franchise, that company no longer exists and people I work with in the personal development industry, who have no idea of my previous involvement in it, often cite it as lacking in integrity and authenticity and not being what it claimed to be. Whilst I feel happier knowing that my gut instinct was right, it doesn't give me any satisfaction in knowing that neither of these businesses have been successful or as successful as they could have been. All it does is sadden me that the individuals at the helm couldn't have been open and honest and not just focused on the money they could make.

Through my own personal growth and personal development, I have learned that success is so much more than material wealth and in pursuing happiness and fulfilment in all areas of your life you are much more likely to succeed financially.

Whilst pursing what I believed was my purpose; to speak from the stage to help others by sharing my experiences and expertise; I got glimpses of my own happiness and fulfilment, integrity and authenticity. Unfortunately, I hadn't aligned my goals and methods of achievement with people who were completely on the same page as I was. This was going to come with the next rewrite of my script.

One of the biggest learnings I've had whilst writing this book is that you can achieve anything you really want to and alongside your own passion and motivation the best way of doing that is to "upgrade your peer group". It's one of the key messages from a conference I attended and subscribes to the popular thought that you become the same or similar to the five people you spend the most time with. Therefore, if you spend time with negative, inauthentic people who are lacking in integrity they will have some influence on you and your thoughts and behaviour. They will also jar against your own values creating the niggling feeling in the back or your mind or in the pit of your stomach. On the other hand, if they are passionate, open, honest and genuine individuals who care about others as much as themselves, then you too will flourish like them.

If I could share just one thing about business, career, passion or purpose it would be to surround yourself with people who are like you or better. That is people who share the same mindset as you, who want you to succeed and are further along the path than you are. Get yourself the right Agent, Manager and Publicist for you. Work alongside people who will help you to achieve your goal, pursue your passion and deliver your dream in way that resonates with you.

And remember, you might have setbacks along the road but as long as you have set your vision, and my vision never changed, then you will get there. My vision has always remained the same, to get on stage and speak or perform. At the moment, I'm focusing on speaking, writing and on being me, the real authentic me who speaks with integrity and from experience. That's far more fulfilling than putting on a performance and being the person other people want me to be.

CHAPTER 7

Therapist, Personal Trainer and Chef - Health and Wellness

Whilst trying to sort my head out and get some stability in my life, I also knew that I had to look at my health and wellbeing. I had seriously neglected myself. Whilst I was married and had my first business I had survived pretty much on black coffee, wine and cooked breakfasts and when I was on my own my self-care hadn't really improved.

I was surviving on wine, water, fruit and crisps with the occasional bag of chips or pizza thrown in. Occasionally I'd make soup but it was all about what was quick and easy, although I did make an effort to cook a proper meal at weekends when Sam was with me. I knew I wasn't helping myself; with severe allergies to wheat, cow's milk and soya I was running a major self-sabotage pattern.

Things came to a head one evening when I'd ordered a pizza for Sam. I missed pizza and there was nothing nicer than the pizzas that were delivered to the door. They were just as pizzas should be and the shop-bought, home-baked pizzas weren't the same. Gluten-free pizzas were just like cardboard. There were times that I just had to have pizza.

I'm sure you've been like that too. You know you shouldn't have that extra slice of cake but you just have to have it! That's where I was at with the pizza that day!

Despite being severely allergic to the majority of the ingredients I had never suffered with anaphylactic shock and had never been diagnosed as coeliac so I would often tell myself that by having just one sandwich, one slice of pizza, one piece of cake I was actually helping myself to bolster my immune system and decrease my potential future allergic reactions.

My reactions always took and still take the same form, if I'd eaten wheat my stomach would swell up almost immediately, making me look at least 8 months pregnant within about 20 minutes, I'd get breathless and my throat would tighten and I'd get severe stomach pains and discomfort.

If I'd had cow's milk or soya I developed cold-type symptoms within minutes; runny nose, sneezes, sore throat and a constant frog in my throat.

Nothing life-threatening but enough to render me helpless and had in the past hospitalised me for 3 days whilst the healthcare professionals tried to decide which of my internal organs was actually causing the problem, checking everything except my colon or my diet.

On this one occasion, having had a pizza delivered as a treat for Sam, I just couldn't resist pinching a slice that he hadn't been able to eat after he had gone to bed. He was only about 8 at the time so it was well before 9pm. I'd called my friend for one of our regular catch ups, we'd often sit watching a TV programme whilst on the phone with a drink or pizza each but in our own homes.

I poured a glass of wine, turned on the TV and grabbed a slice of pizza. As our conversation went on my friend asked. "Are you alright?"

"Yes" I replied "Why?"

"Well your voice sounds strange, you sound as if you've got your mouth full, are you eating?"

"Not now, I had a slice of pizza just as we got on the phone but I haven't had anything since then."

"Was it a normal pizza?"

"Yes."

"Why are you eating that? You know you're allergic."

"I know but I couldn't resist."

The last comment was almost incomprehensible as I felt my tongue seemingly take over my mouth. Sometimes it takes someone else to point out what is blatantly obvious as we choose to ignore what we know we shouldn't.

I'd been getting as breathless as usual but hadn't really paid attention to the fact that my tongue was swelling. My friend had sensed it almost instantly as my usually clear voice had sounded slightly muffled.

The penny dropped and I spent the next half an hour drinking water whilst my friend was on the phone ensuring my tongue didn't swell anymore and I didn't lose consciousness. I'd been self-sabotaging for months. I'd never done anything that stupid with Sam in the house but I realised that I was on a slippery slope and if I didn't do something now I might go too far.

I'd previously taken the decision that I wanted to stay around to be there for Sam when he grew up yet her I was subconsciously trying to sabotage my very existence.

I thought things might improve when Michael moved in with me. I didn't want him to think I was a 'fruitcake' and from the start I told him about my allergies and what I could and couldn't eat. With hindsight I was simply putting the burden of responsibility onto him so I still wasn't looking after myself.

We have a tendency to do that when our self-esteem and self-confidence are low. We try to make our wellbeing someone else's responsibility which is grossly unfair to them and of no help at all to us.

However, whilst Michael ensured I avoided what I was allergic to and took over the cooking to ensure that I ate proper meals it wasn't long before I was piling on weight. In just over a year I went from a UK dress size 10/12 to a 14/16 and increasing. I wasn't exercising and I wasn't paying attention to what I was eating.

Michael, in a bid to look after me, had researched lots of lovely things that I could eat and would come home laden with delicatessen meats, goat and sheep cheese and packets of the latest 'free from' products he'd spotted on the supermarket shelves.

With very little fruit and vegetables in the mix my diet quickly became full of saturated fats that I'd never eaten before to that extent. I have a photograph of me during this time that I stumbled across some 3 years later. It was taken as we were out for a meal for Sam's 8th birthday, not long before Michael and I split up.

I was scrolling through my phone looking for a photograph that I knew had been taken around that time, before I found what I was looking for, I came across a photo of a woman I didn't recognise. And when I say that I didn't recognise her I mean I genuinely looked at the photo and asked myself "Who's that?" until I realised that there was something vaguely familiar about her, and then the realisation dawned that it was me. I'm happy to say that I look nothing like that woman now and look everything like 'me'.

I knew enough about cooking and taking care of myself to know logically that I was eating the wrong things and the weight was piling on. I'd always been a busy active person but since Michael and I got together I'd spend my evenings after dinner, sat on the sofa, watching whatever was on TV whilst sharing a bottle or two of wine and eating whatever treats he'd brought home with him.

The correlation between self-care, self-esteem and self-confidence wasn't lost on me but somehow, I didn't make the link, or rather I chose not to make the link. Each time I tried to improve my diet or do some exercise I was easily swayed by the temptation of something not good for me. Rather than say 'no' to Michael, I would just take whatever was offered to keep him happy. Instead of making the changes I knew I needed to make, I believed that if I didn't address them they didn't exist.

The legacy of these few years of self-neglect didn't show itself until after I met Alun.

Having changed just about everything else I decided it was also time to start looking after myself, made easier by living with someone who liked to eat simple healthy food, exercise (he was running ultra-marathons and marathons at the time) and drink in moderation. However, with my new diet and exercise regime (nothing major, just the occasional circuits class and some lengths of the local pool), I started to regain awareness of my body and my body was determined to let me know that I'd mistreated it badly.

Within 6 months of meeting and moving in with Alun I was on a cancer fast-track after a routine visit to my GP has resulted in a scan which showed a growth on an ovary. Less than 3 hours after the scan the GP had telephoned me at home and asked to see me in her surgery at 9am the following morning.

I was terrified.

Whilst not ruling cancer in or out and referring to what had been spotted as a growth or a mass which may or may not be benign I was referred to the local gynaecological oncology consultant. I was advised that the only solution was a total hysterectomy which would mean the removal of my uterus, fallopian tubes, both ovaries and surrounding tissue – just to be on the safe side!

Less than two months after my visit to the GP I was on the operating table awaiting my fate. The surgery went well although had to be converted to open surgery mid procedure as the growth was too big to remove via keyhole surgery. I awoke sometime after, incredibly groggy and unable to move.

Alun was at my bedside looking relieved and stayed there for quite some while as I came around properly – I had given him and the nurses a shock when my blood-pressure had dipped so low that I flat-lined for a few seconds shortly after being transferred to the ward from the recovery room.

I recall lying in my comatose state thinking, "Someone's in trouble, their machine is making a racket, that's not good" when that 'someone' was actually me and it was my own monitor that was 'making a racket'! I guess it was as close as I got to an out of body experience.

It would be another week before I was told that the growth wasn't ovarian cancer as they'd suspected and was in fact the "worst case of endometriosis that my consultant had ever seen in all her years of surgery".

I'd had 'women's problems' ever since my periods started at the age of 12, regular visits to the GP and subsequent hospital examinations and explorations had failed to diagnose the endometriosis that my Consultant told me was the definite cause of my previous seven miscarriages. She was actually surprised that I'd managed to have a child at all!

This was the wake-up call I really needed to take my health seriously. My recuperation was long, painful and boring. I started writing poetry, mainly drug-induced, whilst I was still bed-bound and my creativity returned. By then I truly recognised the importance of putting the right foods into my body. I knew that if I wanted to hasten my recovery I had to give my body the goodness it needed. That meant fresh fruit and vegetables, fresh meat, fresh fish, gluten free bread and pasta (if I was having any at all) and wine in moderation. After just a few days my body started to respond. I had energy, I was sleeping well and I was recovering fast. I was even able to get out and about and walk a few steps.

All change has to start somewhere, and I decided that whilst I wasn't physically capable of making massive changes or going for a run around the block, I could set myself a small goal to accomplish each day, recognising that small incremental steps create massive change in the long run

Initially, my goal was just being able to walk around the flat unaided, then it was going up and down the stairs, then walking to the corner of the road, then to the end of the road. I employed all of the same tactics that I'd used to get me off my kitchen floor and back into the world all those years ago.

Slowly but surely, I was changing my mindset and giving myself proof that I could achieve my goals. We do that don't we? We convince ourselves that we can't do something when if we just stop and think we find that we have lots of evidence that we are capable of achieving our goals. What evidence have you got that you can and will achieve your goals?

Prior to surgery I had been bemoaning the fact that I couldn't find a job and wasn't going to get invited to interview even if I did find one. 6-weeks after surgery I was able to drive myself to a job interview and successfully get the job.

A minor tactic, to get me walking around again, had

ultimately impacted on other areas of my life. What little tactics can you employ to help you get out of the wings and closer to your spotlight?

Funnily enough, I realised that the stability of a job might be just what I needed to alleviate some of the stress I'd been holding onto for years.

Since then I have taken up running, I joined my local running club's beginner's course '10k in 10 Weeks'. At the first meeting/run I really didn't think 10k in 10 weeks was feasible and set myself the goal of just being able to run a mile without being too out of breath in 10 weeks.

Needless to say, 10 weeks later, at the age of 44, I completed my first 10k in 1 hour 12 minutes. Proof if ever it was needed that taking small steps on a regular basis can certainly help you to realise your goals and dreams. Not that running 10k had been a particular goal but improving my fitness was.

However, my body was still reeling from the years of chronic stress I had subjected it to. 2 years after my hysterectomy I suffered a gallstones attack and had my gall bladder removed but two weeks after keyhole surgery I was back running again. My fitness was definitely improving and this surgery was only a minor blip.

I went on to do two more 10k races, improving my time in each race before suffering a hip injury, fractured pelvis and pulling my Achilles tendon. However, I proved to myself that with the right attitude and small achievable and measurable goals, I was capable of doing things I'd always said I could never do. Whilst I'm still off proper running due to the Achilles injury, I still manage to run a mile or two a couple of times a week. Slowly but surely, I am building up my speed and distance.

Diet and exercise have seen my dress size reduce back

down to a UK 10/12, whilst I don't run as much as I was doing I still enjoy it and I walk further. The running has meant that our walking holidays are much easier as I don't get out of breath, because I'm exercising regularly. I prefer to eat healthier food and I drink less now than I've drunk at any point in my adult life.

Now, if I don't do some exercise in a week I miss it. If I don't eat healthily my body feels sluggish and I feel groggy. I've learned to listen to my body and give it what it needs rather than what it craves. Although I am rather partial to gluten free ginger biscuits but one box of 8 biscuits lasts me a week! All things in moderation. A little bit of what you fancy does you good as my mother would say!

I treat myself to a fortnightly massage. I opt for head, neck and shoulders or a foot massage depending on my mood or what my body indicates it needs. I get my hair done at the local salon rather than doing it myself as I used to and I invest in the Arbonne skincare and cosmetics that I really love rather than buying the cheapest on the shelf.

And I still do all of this on a budget by using life-hacking strategies to enable me to be the best I can be.

Looking after myself has had an unexpected impact across all other areas of my life.

It has improved my self-esteem and self-confidence which in turn has had an impact on all of the relationships in my life and my outlook on life.

And this is just the beginning.

I am only just stepping out of the wings and into MY spotlight.

In the exercises in Finale of this book, I give you the tools you need to make the same changes. Starting with one small action every day. If you choose to just change 1 thing per month, at the end of a year you will have made 12 changes which will have a far-reaching impact on your life.

We all need a helping hand and this is my way of helping you.

Are you ready to step out of the wings into YOUR spotlight? Let's do this!

CHAPTER 8

Accountant and Wealth Manager - Financial

One of the biggest lessons I've had to learn has been around money. Going through bankruptcy was a sobering experience. Although I didn't have huge personal debt I'd always lived slightly beyond my means, going into my overdraft every month and always managing to spend just a little bit more on my credit card each month. My mother had been a building society manager before she retired and she regularly despaired of me ever getting to grips with money. I've always been a 'live for today' person and believed that 'something will come along' when thinking about the future.

Bankruptcy changed all that. First of all, I had no choice but to live a frugal existence, at one stage I had absolutely no income and had to somehow or other eke out what little money I had managed to accumulate. Over time this became a game and I surprised myself with how creative I could become with what little I had. I've got a number of information sheets and e-books written around the subject because for me it was a time of enlightenment. All of these are available on my website www.notarehearsal.co.uk. All the years that my mother's words about saving for a rainy day had fallen on deaf ears and I realised with unsurprising, but remarkable clarity that she was right. Isn't mum usually right?

Do you find that happens to you too? You hear your mother's voice confirming that what she's been telling you all along is right. We all do it. You're not alone. Let's just acknowledge that mums know a thing or two. Thanks Mum x.

If I had paid attention, saved some of my money, things might not have been quite so tight when I was bankrupt but there was no point in fretting over it. I had to get on and make the best of how things were and use where I was as a starting point.

It sounds strange but I had incredible focus and clarity at the time. I had a limited pot of money, no access to any credit and I had a number of commitments to be met. It's surprising how by applying boundaries and limits, voluntarily or having them imposed upon you, can make you work things out. It wasn't easy by any stretch of the imagination and there was a while where I survived for a week on bowls full of Tesco Value porridge oats made with water. They cost 45p for a 1kg bag. They were fuel, nothing more, nothing less. They provided me with the sustenance to keep going for a number of days and I reminded myself that at least I could eat a couple of bowls of them per day, feeling grateful that I wasn't a refugee in an African state, wondering where the next mouthful was coming from.

Thankfully, days of such stringent frugality, were few and far between but they made me realise that I was capable of anything if I only set my mind to it and with that mind-set I made a plan once more.

We are all capable of so much more than we think we are. You are far more capable of achieving whatever you set your mind to than you currently think. Work with me through the exercises in Finale, step out of the wings into your spotlight and see just what you're capable of. You'll be pleasantly surprised.

I had read many books and heard numerous personal development speakers talk about paying yourself first. I vowed that for every bit of income I received I would save a minimum of 10%. In reality I was only saving coppers in a jar on a shelf in my lounge for quite some time because I just didn't have enough money coming in to save anywhere near 10%. Some days even putting the coppers in the jar was leaving me short of a few pence to buy bread for Sam or a tin of beans. But the actual act of putting money aside for me was what was really important. Remember what I said earlier about 'acting as if'. This was just another part of developing the character and becoming who I wanted to be. We're all able to 'act as if'. You can do the same too by taking a small step towards your spotlight.

The ritual of emptying the coppers out of my purse each Friday evening is something I still do and it's surprising how those coppers mount up. Whereas previously I actually used those coppers to buy something I needed, now I save them up all year around and take Sam to play the penny slot machines at the nearby seaside. We spend one Sunday afternoon counting them out into neat £1 piles and then the following weekend we take a small number of them, usually about £5 each, no more than that, and have fun feeding the greedy slots. We see how much we can make, both of us with our own strategies on how the other can capitalise on their expenditure and when the best time is to let go of the coin in the slot! Sometimes we bring some coppers back home but usually we end up feeding them all to the machines. It's a lovely way to spend some quality time together without worrying about spending too much money and has become a summer ritual we both look forward to. However, I'm sure by the time he's 15 it won't be cool to be getting excited about putting coppers into the push-penny machines with his mum! But he's currently 13 and is looking forward to it this summer but has already given me the caveat that he might arrange to meet his friends afterwards so I'll probably have to go home without him!

Getting into the habit of putting money away was something I really needed to get used to. As a child I had always managed to save and somehow, the less money I had, the further I made it stretch. As soon as I started earning a regular income I seemed to forget how to budget and manage my money and believed that it would last forever, regularly treating myself to little inexpensive niceties that once upon a time I'd saved up for a number of weeks to get.

Of course, the odd £5, £10 or £20 here and there soon mounts up and before I knew it I had lots of month left and no money. With hindsight, I'm surprised I didn't end up in serious financial trouble earlier and whilst the bankruptcy was triggered by my business failing it could very easily have happened to me years earlier by my own personal financial mismanagement.

We all do things like that and if managing your finances is one of the things you want to change then you can do it too. Like I've said, small daily changes will soon make a big impact. Look at the exercises and worksheets in Finale, commit to stepping out of the wings into your spotlight and you'll soon be seeing the same sort of results that I had. If I can do it, anyone can. I'm just a normal working mum trying to juggle everything life throws at me. We all go through it. We all make mistakes, that's human nature. You don't have to let your mistakes define your future, you can use them to inform and change your future.

Understandably I have since paid a lot of attention to what comes in and what goes out, of my purse and my bank accounts. I don't always have much, if any, left at the end of the month but I do, somehow or other, manage to make it balance and everything that must be paid, is paid. Anything else is not a necessity and if I want it badly enough I will save for it and buy it when the money is there.

My money mind-set is an ongoing learning curve and just as I think I've got it sorted something will come along from left field and scupper my plans. It will wipe out what little savings I've managed to accumulate at the time and I will have to start again, but at least I do start again, knowing that it is possible to make ends meet, have a pretty good life on a budget, save up for what I really want and have money left at the end of the month rather than too much month at the end of the money.

It's an ongoing challenge but I can at least now take a step back, reflect on where I was and create a vision of where I want to be. Getting to where I want to be is achievable, one step at a time. Of course, like many things, if you want to make a change it helps to have someone guiding or advising you. Over the years I have gleaned lots of advice from various money advisors, websites, TV programmes, podcasts and the like and the majority of them say the same things in their own way;

Live within your means - don't spend more than you earn.

Pay off high interest credit first.

Make sure you know what your income and expenditure actually is.

Pay yourself first.

Save for what you want rather than succumbing to instant gratification.

Do your food shopping with a list

All such basic common-sense advice but so many of us choose to ignore it for the thrill of instant gratification which lasts only moments and takes months or years to pay off.

Knowing where you want to be and having a financial goal really can help to focus your mind. You don't have to want to be a millionaire. Great if you do and you achieve that, but there's nothing wrong with having different financial goals either. I've found that with finances more than any other area of my life, having a realistic goal means I'm more likely to stick to my plans. Yes, I'd love to not have to worry about money but because I'm not actually that bothered about becoming a millionaire, as long as I have enough to do what I want to do, paying an extra £10 into the savings pot each month doesn't feel as if it's making much of a difference. However, when my goal is 'booking a nice holiday next year using savings not a credit card' it suddenly makes it much more achievable. And before anyone comments about that, I will book it on the credit card to ensure I'm covered by the guarantee but I won't book it until I have the full amount saved up and can transfer that amount to clear my credit card account.

You see, it's not about not using credit cards at all, it's about using them sensibly and responsibly as a purchasing tool rather than a necessity that I buy all of the essentials on.

Mindset shifts like this take some time to get used to and you won't always get it right but knowing when you've made a mistake and knowing how to start again makes a huge difference and makes those little mistakes much easier to handle and overcome. We're looking at changing habits. It takes 28 days for a habit to become embedded in our neural pathways so by choosing to step out of the wings into the spotlight and take one small step every day for a month, you will slowly create a new habit. Give it a go and see how it feels. It's a bit like trying on a costume for the first time. Until you try it you won't know if it fits. What will your character, the new 'you' do?

It will also help you if you can identify a good financial advisor, if you can't afford or don't want to speak to an Independent Chartered advisor who can help you to plan for your future, you can always start by speaking to your bank, just be aware that your bank will only talk to you about the products they offer and might have sales targets they need to meet so don't say yes to a financial product just because you feel pressurised into signing up for it. Take the time you need to reach a decision and do a little more shopping around.

There is also the Money Personal Trainer. A fabulous group on Facebook set up by my money mentor and good friend, Clare Turner Marshall. She offers excellent advice in the group, via webinars, on her website and in a membership group. Take a look at www.themoneypt.com you won't be disappointed.

It's taken a long time for me to appreciate the importance of various financial products and mechanisms. I'm still learning which are the most appropriate for me and which I'm aspiring to become involved in, invest in or purchase. In the meantime I've done a lot of research, asked lots of questions and identified those people I want to be part of my financial team, my financial advisor(s) and wealth planner(s) for a start and if Sam's current career plan is still his goal when he's older then I'll have a personal stock-broker too!

Money has been one of my biggest issues and lack of it has been a significant contributor to many of my problems but the more I learn about it, the fewer problems I have. You're never too old to learn and if you learn nothing else, getting mastery of your money is probably the priority.

As an absolute minimum list out all of your income and expenditure and see where you can make savings. I know it's a headache and takes ages but it will be a few hours well spent. It's something we all need to do occasionally and you'll feel so much better and so much more in control of things if you do it. It will be one small step out of the wings into your spotlight and you'll notice the change at the end of the month.

Come with me now over the page as we start that journey, let's take that step out of the wings together. Your spotlight is shining brightly and it's time you stood in it and owned it.

ACT III

ACTION! – MOVING FORWARD, WHAT
THE FUTURE HOLDS

"The future belongs to those who prepare for it today"
Malcolm X

CHAPTER 9

Stepping into the Spotlight

My relationship with Alun is everything my previous relationships have not been. For a start, we don't have a huge amount of money. But we have enough and we are happy.

We've recently moved from his bachelor pad into a rented property with a garden. It's ideally situated for us and for the things we do so we're in no rush to tie ourselves down with a huge mortgage on a large house just because that's what society dictates we should be doing at our age (mid 40's).

We have some incredible holidays that I would never have had before; we've been canal boating, walking in the beautiful British countryside across moors and up mountains. We have motorcycled across Europe in the worst weather they'd experienced for years and to Lake Maggiore in Northern Italy via France, Switzerland, Mont Blanc and the Alps. As I write we're planning our holidays for the next year or so which so far include another canal boating trip, another walking holiday, a motorbike adventure to Northern Italy and my usual camping holiday with Sam, my sister and my niece.

We're also contemplating a family skiing holiday and a holiday travelling around Iceland, Tanzania or Costa Rica next summer although Sam is thinking he'd quite like to go sailing instead of skiing! He's developed into quite an adept sailor.

We have date nights which we plan in order to avoid us getting into the same routine week in, week out and we each have our own time pursuing our individual past times and hobbies. We both spend time with Sam as a couple and as individuals and we make plans, and more plans for the future. We go to rock concerts and to the theatre, we watch off the wall debates and documentaries and listen to all sorts of different radio programmes. We both play in a band and we tried and found we rather enjoy ballroom dancing. We try new foods as often as we can and we visit new places. Life is never dull and it's certainly not boring. It's not perfect either if there's such a thing as a perfect life. But it's our life, lived on our terms doing the things we enjoy. It wouldn't suit everyone and we accept that but that's why we're perfect together. This is about us, Sam and no-one else. We both have our own scripts and have written and are continuing to write our joint script.

We all have different scripts depending upon what hat we're wearing at the time. Wife, lover, partner, mother, step-mother, grandmother, daughter, employee, employer, friend, sister. We change our scripts regularly to adapt to changes in our lives. The important thing is to stay true to YOUR script. Know where your spotlight is, keep aiming towards it. Sometimes you will veer to stage left or stage right but know that your spotlight is where you're heading.

No relationship is perfect, we're all individuals and our needs, wants and desires change as we grow older, learn new things and form new opinions and ideas but to be in a relationship where you both respect each other, learn from and grow with each other, is to me, perfect! And most importantly, it's unconditional. We love each other, that's it. Whatever the other might say or do, whatever might happen in our lives, we support each other. Sometimes that's easier said than done and it would be fair to say that we certainly push each other to the limit on occasion but we don't hold grudges. We recognise that it's about give and take with each of us swapping roles as life dishes out whatever it will. We're total opposites yet remarkably similar. We both have unwavering belief in each other and both believe the other person deserves far more success than they think they do.

We all deserve a relationship like that. It took me a very long time to realise that I deserved that but I do. And you do too.

For Alun and I, it's love. It's just that. Sometimes it's hearts, flowers, rainbows and stardust and other times it's grungy, black and terrifying. Sometimes we wonder what on earth we're doing with each other and other times we wonder how we took so long to find each other again. What we both know however, is that now we've found each other, we're going to work mighty hard to make sure we keep each other. This is long haul and it's not always comfortable but we have a firm belief that the destination, whatever that may be will make it all worthwhile and as we are committing to the long-haul we're going to ensure that each chapter is a blockbuster in its own right.

Working through all of this also enabled me to work on my relationship with my parents, my sister and my friends. I have more patience, more compassion and a whole tonne of gratitude to them all for being there for me during those darkest times that I've mentioned briefly in this book but go into more depth about in 'Whatever It Takes'.

My future is looking incredibly bright as I take my position in the centre of my spotlight.

My coaching practice, has launched and having successfully moved myself out the wings into my own spotlight I'm helping countless others do the same too. Monthly rehearsals (coaching groups) are planned to open in different areas, I get invited to speak at events about overcoming adversity, bouncing back and changing the outcome despite the odds, my online coaching programmes are currently being written and my aim is to help lots of other people to step out of the wings into their spotlight by rewriting their scripts to enable them to shine.

When I was going through the darkest moments highlighted in the introduction of this book and detailed in 'Whatever It Takes' it was the thought that one day everything I was going through would help someone else to feel not quite so alone if they were experiencing something similar, that kept me going.

My mantra 'whatever it takes' kept me going.

Whatever you are going through at the moment, I hope you feel encouraged and inspired by my story and it has given you the strength to do whatever it takes to step out of the wings into YOUR spotlight and rewrite your script and shine.

You deserve to live a blockbuster life. My wish is that you take your final bow knowing that your life was a box-office success for YOU.

I've not shared my successes because I want to brag. I am a normal working mum who just decided to make a change and to step out of the wings into MY spotlight. If I can create such massive change, I know you can too. I don't always get it right, and that's fine. We're all only human.

As far as I'm concerned, I've been successful, I don't define success by monetary or material wealth, I define it by happiness and contentment and the things I'm looking forward to. We are all different. There are plenty of people out there who will look at my life and regard me as unsuccessful and having achieved nothing, that's fine too. We all have different levels of success and achievement but the route to success and achievement starts with me, you, us.

However, *you* choose to define your own personal success is perfect for you. There is no right or wrong. You *can* choose how you want to feel and how you want to measure your success. I am just giving you the tools in the Finale to enable you to rewrite your script, create that success and stand in and revel in the brilliance of the spotlight. You've spent too long in the wings, it's time to claim your rightful place in the spotlight of your own life.

FINALE

TIME TO REAP THE REWARDS

"If you really want something, and really work hard, and take advantage of opportunities, and never give up, you will find a way"

Jane Goodall

"Change your thoughts and you change your world"

Norman Vincent Peale

CHAPTER 10

To Now and the Future

This section is purposefully short. The script for my blockbuster life is still being refined, as it will continue to be refined as my life, this story, progresses. I know what I want it to look, feel and sound like but I'm purposefully keeping if flexible so that I can work with plot twists or dramatic interludes as a I choose. Being my own scriptwriter enables me to do that.

It also means that I can learn from the many lessons I've been taught from the experiences I've had to date, good and bad. The key lessons for me are;

Trust your instincts – they are rarely wrong.

Know your boundaries and don't allow anyone to step over them, regardless of who they are.

Know your self-worth.

You are enough. You are good enough, strong enough, beautiful enough, thin enough, smart enough.   You are enough.

Keep fighting for what you believe, even if others think you're mad!

Remain open to new opportunities, new ways of thinking and new methodologies.

From every experience comes a new opportunity for at least one area of your life.

Know that behind the public mask there is always a private face.

Please remember that none of us will have the same blockbuster life and I'm sure neither would we want to. Most lives have a mix of fantastic and joyous events and deeply distressing and disturbing experiences.

Before wishing your life was the same as someone else's ask yourself what their backstory is. What have they had to endure to create their own blockbuster life? What is their public mask hiding?The exercises and worksheets included will help you to write your new script to create your blockbuster life.

I have formalised the steps I took to step out of the wings into the spotlight across all areas of my life which I hope you will find useful. Use them all if you wish or just use those that appeal to you or a certain area of your life. There are no rules.

It is up to you to define the rules of your life and to live it according to your own rules, as long as you don't allow your rules to stifle you.

These exercises and worksheets are designed to give you clarity but are not meant to be followed religiously, this is YOUR script, and you are your own scriptwriter. Over time you will become your own Director and Producer as well, but until then these will help you in rehearsal as you refine your script and hone your performance. If you need support from a Director or Producer then please feel free to get in touch. My contact details are at the end of this book. But for now, work through these exercise, see them as rehearsal preparation and start to move out of the wings into YOUR spotlight.I'm so excited for you. I can't wait to see you in that spotlight.

CHAPTER 11

Worksheets and Exercises

There are numerous themes that have recurred throughout my life and in these exercises and worksheets I have endeavoured to capture them and find a way to work through them or use them to my benefit and including them here is my gift to you to help you rewrite your script, step out of the wings and into YOUR spotlight

As you see from reading both my old script and my new script, time and time again my instincts have always proven to be correct. Even when I've ignored them hindsight has shown that my first gut instinct was the right one. When completing any of these exercises I implore you to follow your gut instinct even if your logical mind is telling you otherwise! These exercises form the very first draft outline of your new script, without them you can't refine or draft your blockbuster life, they are for your eyes only and will kick-start your creativity.

They are included in the order in which I used these tools

to change my life and rewrite my script. For me, this was the logical
order but after doing the first exercise you may wish to focus on a different area first.

There is no right or wrong way, all I ask is that you commit to doing them, only then can you start to rewrite your script, step out of the wings and into YOUR spotlight.

Let's start with working out where you are right now. This is always the hardest part because we always want to jump ahead a few steps to where the magic happens don't we. Well unfortunately, even A-listers have to do the background and research to understand their character's back story and that's what this exercise is all about.

Turn the page and follow the instructions to find out just how far into the wings you are or how close to your spotlight you are. It shouldn't take you any more than a couple of minutes but if you really want to find out the back story why not sit and reflect a while, grab a notebook and pen and make some notes on each section as you start to plot your script.

All of these exercises and worksheets are available on my website:

www.notarehearsal.co.uk/blockbusterlife/downloads.

AM I IN THE WINGS OR IN THE SPOTLIGHT?

Using the spotlight below, take each quarter in turn and ask yourself how happy you are in that area of your life. Rate it on a scale of 0 to 10, where 0 is desperately unhappy and 10 is 'couldn't be happier'. Then taking a felt tip pen, draw an arc at the level you feel you're at then colour in the area between it and the number 10. So if you scored a 7 in career, colour in the gap between 7 and 10, leaving 0 to 7 uncoloured. How much of the spotlight is still showing when you've coloured each quarter? That's how much you're allowing your light to shine. The coloured areas show how much you're hiding your spotlight from others. The quarter where you score the lowest is the area you need to start working on first.

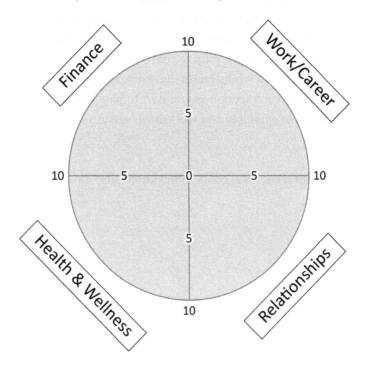

MINDSET: TINY STEPS

It's perfectly normal to feel like you're taking two steps forward and 3 steps back which is why I put this diagram in to reassure you. We start in the Wings and work our way forward through downstage, to upstage and into the spotlight but along the way something might happen that pushes us back one step or two but we rarely end up back exactly where we started. Next time you feel like you're back in the wings or at 'square 1' take a look at this to remind yourself just how far you've come.

January

This month's goals to get me closer to the Spotlight

Within each spotlight pick just one or two goals that you'd like to complete by the end of this month. Don't worry about the how or the what, just list what you'd like to complete. You might have one goal per spotlight or a couple of goals for two or three spotlights. This is YOUR blockbuster life you're planning, what you put in is up to you.

Finance - Accountant

Work/Career - Agent, Manager, Publicist

Health & Wellness - Therapist, Personal Trainer & Chef

Relationships - Supporting Cast & Crew

January

My Daily Steps out of the wings into the SPOTLIGHT

In each spotlight write 1 action you are going to take
TODAY to take you closer to YOUR SPOTLIGHT.

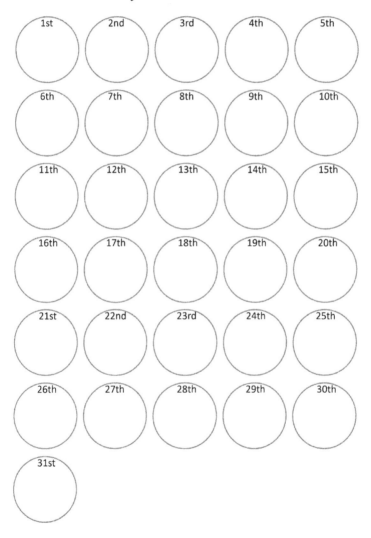

February

This month's goals to get me closer to the Spotlight

Within each spotlight pick just one or two goals that you'd like to complete by the end of this month. Don't worry about the how or the what, just list what you'd like to complete. You might have one goal per spotlight or a couple of goals for two or three spotlights. This is YOUR blockbuster life you're planning, what you put in is up to you.

Finance - Accountant

Work/Career - Agent, Manager, Publicist

Health & Wellness - Therapist, Personal Trainer & Chef

Relationships - Supporting Cast & Crew

February

My Daily Steps out of the wings into the SPOTLIGHT

In each spotlight write 1 action you are going to take
TODAY to take you closer to YOUR SPOTLIGHT.

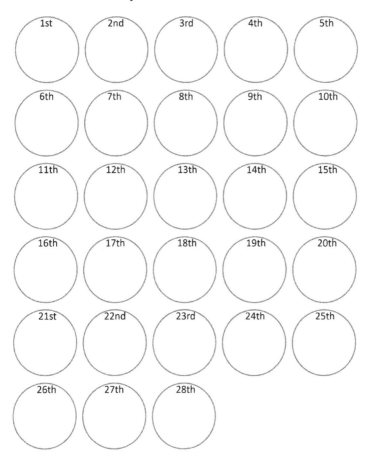

March

This month's goals to get me closer to the Spotlight

Within each spotlight pick just one or two goals that you'd like to complete by the end of this month. Don't worry about the how or the what, just list what you'd like to complete. You might have one goal per spotlight or a couple of goals for two or three spotlights. This is YOUR blockbuster life you're planning, what you put in is up to you.

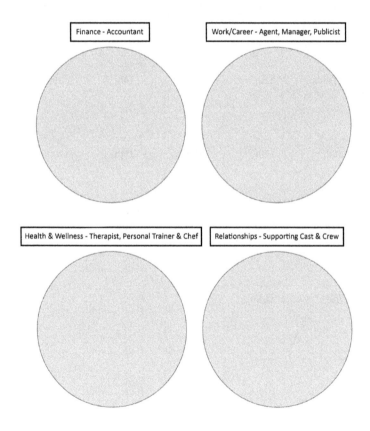

Finance - Accountant

Work/Career - Agent, Manager, Publicist

Health & Wellness - Therapist, Personal Trainer & Chef

Relationships - Supporting Cast & Crew

March

My Daily Steps out of the wings into the SPOTLIGHT

In each spotlight write 1 action you are going to take
TODAY to take you closer to YOUR SPOTLIGHT.

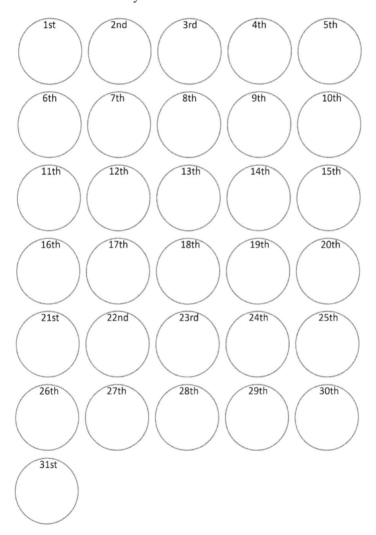

April

This month's goals to get me closer to the Spotlight

Within each spotlight pick just one or two goals that you'd like to complete by the end of this month. Don't worry about the how or the what, just list what you'd like to complete. You might have one goal per spotlight or a couple of goals for two or three spotlights. This is YOUR blockbuster life you're planning, what you put in is up to you.

Finance - Accountant

Work/Career - Agent, Manager, Publicist

Health & Wellness - Therapist, Personal Trainer & Chef

Relationships - Supporting Cast & Crew

April

My Daily Steps out of the wings into the SPOTLIGHT

In each spotlight write 1 action you are going to take
TODAY to take you closer to YOUR SPOTLIGHT.

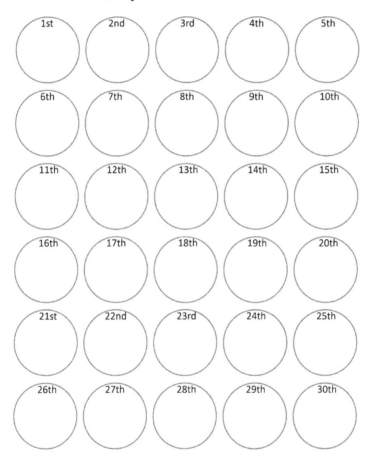

May

This month's goals to get me closer to the Spotlight

Within each spotlight pick just one or two goals that you'd like to complete by the end of this month. Don't worry about the how or the what, just list what you'd like to complete. You might have one goal per spotlight or a couple of goals for two or three spotlights. This is YOUR blockbuster life you're planning, what you put in is up to you.

Finance - Accountant

Work/Career - Agent, Manager, Publicist

Health & Wellness - Therapist, Personal Trainer & Chef

Relationships - Supporting Cast & Crew

May

My Daily Steps out of the wings into the SPOTLIGHT

In each spotlight write 1 action you are going to take
TODAY to take you closer to YOUR SPOTLIGHT.

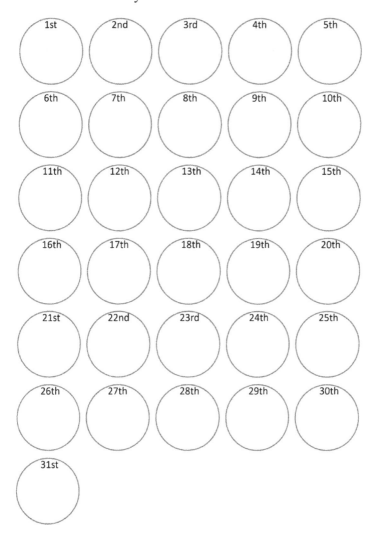

June

This month's goals to get me closer to the Spotlight

Within each spotlight pick just one or two goals that you'd like to complete by the end of this month. Don't worry about the how or the what, just list what you'd like to complete. You might have one goal per spotlight or a couple of goals for two or three spotlights. This is YOUR blockbuster life you're planning, what you put in is up to you.

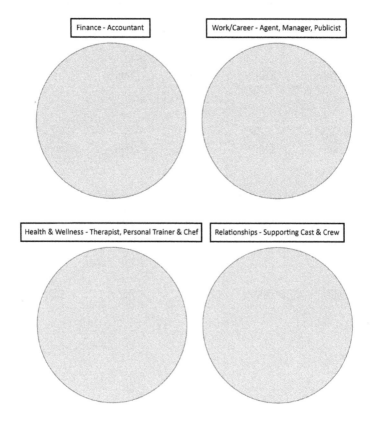

Finance - Accountant

Work/Career - Agent, Manager, Publicist

Health & Wellness - Therapist, Personal Trainer & Chef

Relationships - Supporting Cast & Crew

June

My Daily Steps out of the wings into the SPOTLIGHT

In each spotlight write 1 action you are going to take
TODAY to take you closer to YOUR SPOTLIGHT.

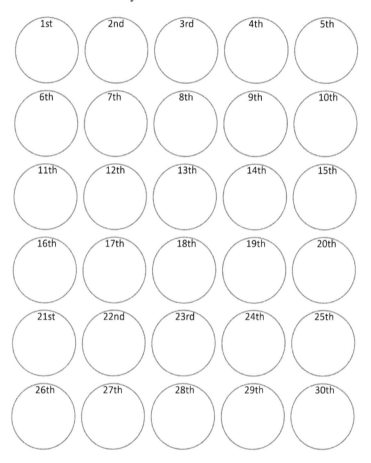

July

This month's goals to get me closer to the Spotlight

Within each spotlight pick just one or two goals that you'd like to complete by the end of this month. Don't worry about the how or the what, just list what you'd like to complete. You might have one goal per spotlight or a couple of goals for two or three spotlights. This is YOUR blockbuster life you're planning, what you put in is up to you.

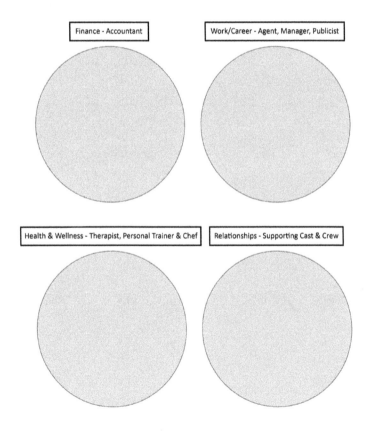

July

My Daily Steps out of the wings into the SPOTLIGHT

In each spotlight write 1 action you are going to take
TODAY to take you closer to YOUR SPOTLIGHT.

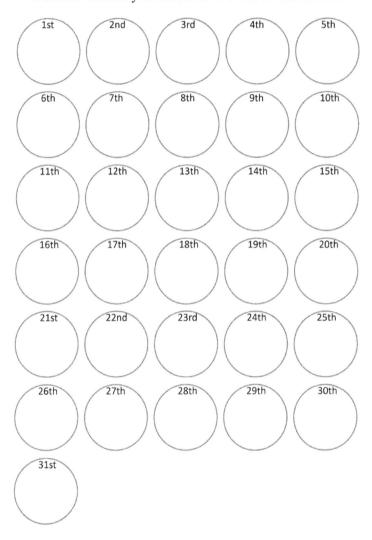

August

This month's goals to get me closer to the Spotlight

Within each spotlight pick just one or two goals that you'd like to complete by the end of this month. Don't worry about the how or the what, just list what you'd like to complete. You might have one goal per spotlight or a couple of goals for two or three spotlights. This is YOUR blockbuster life you're planning, what you put in is up to you.

Finance - Accountant

Work/Career - Agent, Manager, Publicist

Health & Wellness - Therapist, Personal Trainer & Chef

Relationships - Supporting Cast & Crew

August

My Daily Steps out of the wings into the SPOTLIGHT

In each spotlight write 1 action you are going to take
TODAY to take you closer to YOUR SPOTLIGHT.

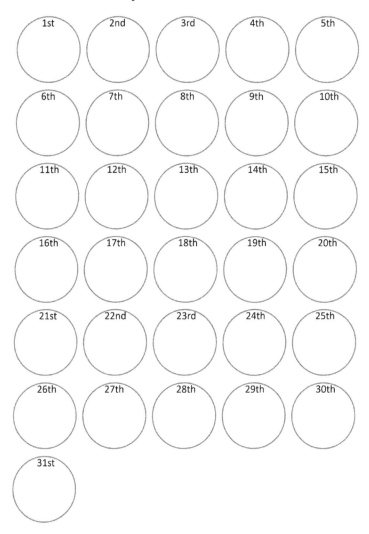

September

This month's goals to get me closer to the Spotlight

Within each spotlight pick just one or two goals that you'd like to complete by the end of this month. Don't worry about the how or the what, just list what you'd like to complete. You might have one goal per spotlight or a couple of goals for two or three spotlights. This is YOUR blockbuster life you're planning, what you put in is up to you.

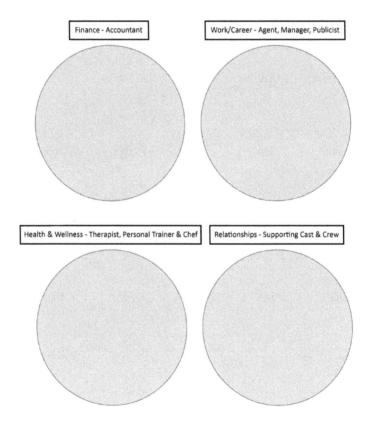

Finance - Accountant

Work/Career - Agent, Manager, Publicist

Health & Wellness - Therapist, Personal Trainer & Chef

Relationships - Supporting Cast & Crew

September

My Daily Steps out of the wings into the SPOTLIGHT

In each spotlight write 1 action you are going to take
TODAY to take you closer to YOUR SPOTLIGHT.

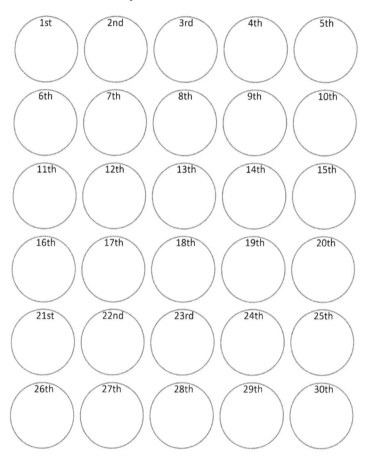

October

This month's goals to get me closer to the Spotlight

Within each spotlight pick just one or two goals that you'd like to complete by the end of this month. Don't worry about the how or the what, just list what you'd like to complete. You might have one goal per spotlight or a couple of goals for two or three spotlights. This is YOUR blockbuster life you're planning, what you put in is up to you.

October

My Daily Steps out of the wings into the SPOTLIGHT

In each spotlight write 1 action you are going to take TODAY to take you closer to YOUR SPOTLIGHT.

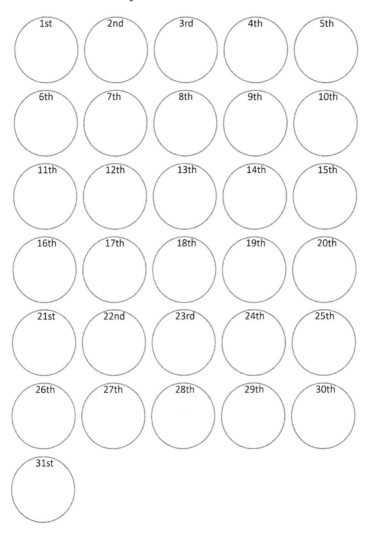

November

This month's goals to get me closer to the Spotlight

Within each spotlight pick just one or two goals that you'd like to complete by the end of this month. Don't worry about the how or the what, just list what you'd like to complete. You might have one goal per spotlight or a couple of goals for two or three spotlights. This is YOUR blockbuster life you're planning, what you put in is up to you.

Finance - Accountant

Work/Career - Agent, Manager, Publicist

Health & Wellness - Therapist, Personal Trainer & Chef

Relationships - Supporting Cast & Crew

November

My Daily Steps out of the wings into the SPOTLIGHT

In each spotlight write 1 action you are going to take
TODAY to take you closer to YOUR SPOTLIGHT.

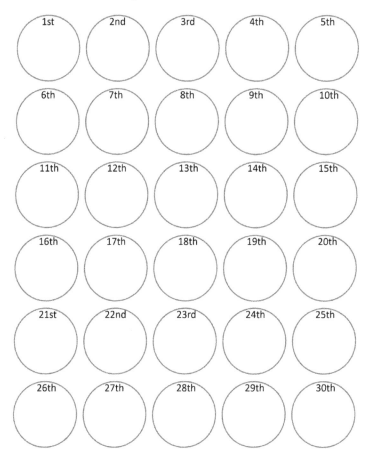

December

This month's goals to get me closer to the Spotlight

Within each spotlight pick just one or two goals that you'd like to complete by the end of this month. Don't worry about the how or the what, just list what you'd like to complete. You might have one goal per spotlight or a couple of goals for two or three spotlights. This is YOUR blockbuster life you're planning, what you put in is up to you.

Finance - Accountant

Work/Career - Agent, Manager, Publicist

Health & Wellness - Therapist, Personal Trainer & Chef

Relationships - Supporting Cast & Crew

December

My Daily Steps out of the wings into the SPOTLIGHT

In each spotlight write 1 action you are going to take TODAY to take you closer to YOUR SPOTLIGHT.

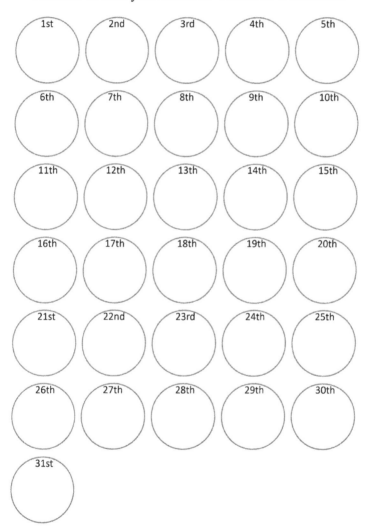

Keep in Touch

How are you getting on? I'm guessing that you've read the book all the way through and are now going to work through the exercises although it's equally possible that you've worked your way through the exercises and have just reached this section. Either way, that's absolutely perfect.

I hope that by sharing my story you feel that you are not alone in rewriting your script. I hope I have inspired you to realise that it's possible to make massive changes by taking tiny steps just as I did.

We always feel a bit apprehensive when we've decided to embark on changes don't we? That's OK. New things always feel a bit strange at first, a bit like putting on a new pair of shoes, you have to break them in for a while! So, put on those shoes you've been dreaming of and start taking a few steps forward, one at a time. You're moving out of the wings now. You're on your way to creating a huge box office hit and stepping firmly into your spotlight. You're sensational. I'd love to hear from you as you step out of the wings into your spotlight. Please share your successes, your script and your blockbuster life with me at **www.notarehearsal.co.uk**.

Why not join me on;

Facebook   NotaRehearsal
Twitter   @not_a_rehearsal
Instagram   lifesnotarehearsal

Be the first to know when I release more coaching dates, launch my next book, plan a speaking tour or add more worksheets and e-books to my website by registering your details at **www.notarehearsal.co.uk**.

I look forward to hearing from you and learning about your blockbuster life.

Together we're going to shine.

Acknowledgments

I am eternally grateful for the people in my life who have been there for me throughout my time in the wings and in the spotlight; mum and dad, who in 50 years of marriage have been by my side constantly. My sister for no-nonsense straight talking, prosecco and camping. My partner, Alun, who always knew the lure of the spotlight would prove too powerful for me to stay in the wings for long. Julie London, Julie Japan, Gel and Sandy all too far away but for being '3am friends'.

To my legal team who have always believed in me; Wayne, Melanie, Judge Price – Thank you.

To my Open University team for increasing my understanding and confidence; Fred, Ana, Julie and Kaye and my tutors over the years who have supported me through breakdowns and breakthroughs.

To Yvette, Clare T-M, Tamsen, Paula, Russ, Tara for reading drafts, providing feedback and being brutally honest but equally gentle with me.

To business contacts who didn't judge and always knew I'd find my spotlight one day; Kerry O, Tamsen, Clare T-M, Brad, Paul H, And people too numerous to mention who supported my various business ventures one way or another.

To Richard for my fabulous artwork ☺

To the best Oncology consultant; Dr Jo Bailey at St Michael's Hospital, Bristol.

To Sue Clay, David Harris, Helen Rule, John Worrall for having faith in me when it mattered.

To Ann, my publisher, who insisted I had 2 books instead of 1 and worked her socks off to make them happen by my self-imposed deadline!

About the Author

The Author has always been someone who gets things done. Her mantras are 'no matter what', 'whatever it takes' and 'there's always a way'.

From being recognised in 2007 by Insider magazine as one of South Wales' "Top 20 Entrepreneurs to Watch" and finding herself sitting on the IOD Wales Management committee the author is all about shining brightly herself and supporting others out of the wings and into their spotlight so they too can shine brightly in their own production.

The author has had her fair share of hiding in the wings and when her industry leading business became insolvent overnight she was plunged into the turmoil of taking her own business through administration and personal bankruptcy. Her second marriage collapsed and she went through three redundancies. She suffered panic attacks, agoraphobia and more. For a while she thought she might stay in the wings forever but the lure of the spotlight proved too much of a draw.

The Author knew that she couldn't (and wouldn't) spend the rest of her life hiding in the wings, she decided she would get back into her spotlight no matter what and whatever it took.

She created a plan, a rehearsal schedule if you like, that enabled her to do just that. Deborah is passionate about enabling other people to create their own rehearsal schedule to move them gently out of the wings into their own spotlight.

The Author now lives the life she has always wanted. She has amazing relationships with the two most important people in her life; her partner and her son. She says, "I have regular holidays and I'm fitter and healthier than I've ever been."

As a coach she helps people move out of the wings into their spotlight so that they can become the star of their own life production. "And as far as I'm concerned, this is just the opening number."